THE GAME
I WON'T
FORGET...
Wisconsin Badgers

THE GAME
I WON'T
FORGET...

Wisconsin Badgers

Mike Beacom

KCI SPORTS PUBLISHING

CREDITS

Copyright© 2010 Mike Beacom

ISBN: 0-9843882-7-3
ISBN 13: 978-0-9843882-7-1

This book is available in quantity at special discounts for your group or organization. For further information, contact:

KCI Sports Publishing
3340 Whiting Avenue
Suite 5
Stevens Point, WI 54481
(217) 766-3390
Fax: (715) 344-2668

Cover Design: Nicky Brillowski
Book Layout and Design: Nicky Brillowski

Photos courtesy of University of Wisconsin Athletic Department

Printed in the United States

ACKNOWLEDGEMENT

I feel fortunate to have done this book with Peter Clark and the rest of the KCI Publishing team. I was comfortable working with Peter on day one and hope this is the first of many projects together.

Much thanks to Barry Alvarez for writing the foreword. Wisconsin is home to a number of sports heroes; Barry is one of its true sports legends.

Thanks to the University of Wisconsin Athletic Department staff, most notably Justin Doherty, Brian Lucas, and the folks at the W Club. I am also grateful to Steve Hill and Josh Wussow for their help on this project.

To my partner, Lisa, and our daughters, Jada and Isis, thanks for your love and support, and for tolerating Big Ten football every Saturday afternoon in the fall.

And a special thanks to the 20 men who lent their stories to this project. It is because of you that this book became possible, but more importantly, it's because of you that Badgers fans can stand proud!

FOREWORD

All football players have a game in their past that they won't ever forget. Maybe their team upset a highly-ranked opponent. Maybe they had an interception or threw a key block on a long touchdown run. Maybe they missed a tackle that cost the team a score. Whatever the reason – good or bad – these games tend to stick with players long after their days on the field are over.

Interestingly, not all of the games discussed in this book are victories. This doesn't surprise me. Sometimes the toughest games to get over are the ones where your team outplayed your opponent yet still lost the game. In 1991, I remember playing Iowa with a lot of young kids, and a bad call negated a touchdown. That could have been a big win for our program, and the memory of that game sticks with me to this day.

The former Badger players included in this book are some of the best to ever step on the field at Camp Randall. I had the pleasure of coaching a number of them. Some were highly-recruited; some flew under the radar. Many went on to success in the NFL. Through their candid discussion of the game they won't forget, Badger fans are able to get a rare glimpse of the preparation and dedication it takes to be successful at this level.

I always enjoy getting together and reminiscing with my Nebraska teammates about our playing days. Each year the touchdown runs get a few yards longer, the tackles more bone-crunching and the wins more impressive. I hope you enjoy reminiscing with the Badger greats and *The Game I Won't Forget.*

Barry Alvarez

CONTENTS

INTRODUCTION

In the summer of 2007, I began searching for former Badger players willing to share the story of their most memorable college football game. More important than featuring the biggest names, the hope was that these players could offer insight into different periods of the program – a collection of individual stories that, tied together, also tells the history of Badger football.

Early on, it became apparent that these men would have more to offer.

Tarek Saleh and Chris McIntosh were the first two players I interviewed. Their personalities couldn't have been more different, yet they clearly were connected by something that went beyond the game of football. Both men spoke of how their lives had been forever changed the day they set foot on the Madison campus. They had experienced highs and lows on the football field, and had collected a closet's worth of hardware for their efforts. But the wins and trophies were secondary; what mattered most to both men were the life lessons they took from their tour of duty.

It's the theme that ties this book together – that unites those young men who played for Wisconsin in the 1950s with those who played for Barry Alvarez's Badger teams a half century later.

The 20 players profiled in this book represent some of the finest players Badger fans have known through the years. Captains, record-breakers and underdogs. All that was asked of each player was a simple question: What was the one game during your time at the University of Wisconsin that stands out the most? A few selected their most productive day in a Badger uniform. A couple picked the game in which they first gained public recognition. Others chose bowl wins or crushing defeats. In each case, it's a game that's had a profound impact on that individual.

Each chapter is designed to provide insight into the players' lives before and after their time at Madison, sandwiched around their tale of that memorable contest. In some cases, there was simply too much to share in a single chapter. Many of these men could fill an entire book (a couple of them already have) and all of them could have selected a handful or more games to speak about. But the focus was kept on that one game – the game they won't forget.

For me, having the opportunity to share in the re-telling of each story – the hours of research and interviews – is an experience I won't forget.

RED WILSON
1946-1949

When Robert 'Red' Wilson glanced over the list of names that had picked positions for the upcoming football season, it was obvious few wanted to play on the offensive line; no one was listed at guard. But Wilson was determined to play for Milwaukee's Washington High School, so, he thought, 'Why not?'

Under the guidance of Lisle Blackbourn, who later coached the Green Bay Packers, Wilson also played linebacker and a little fullback at Washington. "We had a very good team, and a very talented backfield," he says. "All four of our backfield players were speedsters."

Wilson was a multi-sport standout for the school, but football and baseball were his best two sports. Growing up on the streets of Milwaukee, Wilson played whatever baseball he could – first in the City's youth program (all of its teams named after players from the old American Association Milwaukee Brewers club), then in American Legion.

"Initially, my favorite position to play was leftfield," says Wilson. "But one day a neighbor, who at one time played some baseball, dropped off a catcher's mitt at our home after having seen me and my buddies playing in the street. No one else had a catcher's mitt. And so that started off my interest in being a catcher."

Having been converted by Blackbourn to play center his senior season of football, Wilson had caught the eye of one of the University of Wisconsin's Milwaukee-based talent scouts. Wilson went to Madison in 1946 on a football scholarship but relished the idea of playing both sports for the Badgers.

"Football was the more high-profile sport, but baseball was an activity I enjoyed because I didn't want to go out for spring football," he laughs.

During his first year on campus, Wilson was joined by his older brother, Tom, who was fresh from his tours in World War II. The two men lived together and Tom played a little JV football that first year even though he hadn't played in high school.

Wilson didn't start during his freshman season but played quite a bit. The team's starting center, Fred Negus, had been first-team all-conference in 1942 before he had left for the war. When Negus didn't return to the squad in 1947, the job belonged to the 6-foot, 185-pound Wilson.

"Harry Stuhldreher was our coach. A fine person. But his staff consisted of only one full-time assistant, and the rest was made up of individuals who had other responsibilities. It was a situation where the University of Wisconsin football program hadn't kept up with the times. And I played in an era where it was not unusual to go all 60 minutes. Other schools began to change to a two-platoon system in the late '40s – schools like Notre Dame and Michigan – but Wisconsin didn't really get with it until Ivy Williamson arrived."

Already as a sophomore, Wilson had become one of the Big Ten's dominant two-way players, ranking as one of its best centers and most-feared linebackers.

GAME I WON'T FORGET
November 15, 1947
vs Michigan

The Badgers easily beat Purdue, 32-14, before playing to a 7-7 tie against Indiana in Bloomington. The next week the Badgers suffered a 48-7 loss to No. 8 ranked California. It could have derailed the club, but the team refocused and rattled off wins over Yale (9-0), Marquette (35-12), Northwestern (29-0) and Iowa (46-14).

Part of the reason for Wisconsin's turnaround can be attributed to Stuhldreher's open-huddle offense. All of the Badgers plays were called at the line of scrimmage, depending on what the defense gave them to work with. Says Wilson, "I recall vividly that Northwestern used two alignments on defense, and so when we got up to the line of scrimmage and our quarterback called the play, one of our plays worked well against one of their defenses and one worked well against their alternate defense. We had a heyday, if you will."

The Badgers now ranked among the top 10 in the country for the first time since that memorable 1942 season. The next opponent – Fritz Crisler's Michigan Wolverines – was ranked No. 2 thanks to an 11-game winning streak, but everyone in Madison was confident the Badgers could win.

"There was a lot of excitement about our success going into the Michigan game," says Wilson. "We were a much improved team and we had a little more depth than we had had previously."

Wrote Henry J. McCormick in that Friday's *Wisconsin State Journal*, "Never in my experience have I ever seen a team more steamed up over a game than is Wisconsin. They won't be beat for want of trying."

But Wisconsin's desire was not enough to convince outsiders of their chances; the Wolverines were a 13-point favorite and entered the contest with a 6-0-1 career mark in games played at Madison. And with a backfield that possessed two players who would be named All-American that year (Robert Chappuis and Chalmers 'Bump' Elliot) the Wolverines had the better team on paper ... and it showed early in the contest.

Michigan scored the game's first points on a pass from Chappuis to Howard Yerges. Later in the first quarter, Gene Derricotte returned a punt 77 yards to give the Wolverines a 13-0 lead.

When things did start to go well for Wisconsin, something inevitably stalled the momentum. Clarence Self returned the ensuing kick 70 yards to the Michigan 13-yard line, but a few plays later an Earl Girard pass was intercepted by Derricotte in the end zone.

Thanks to another long return by Self, the Badgers began a second quarter possession at the Michigan 41. Several plays later, James Embach took a reverse six yards to give Wisconsin its first score. Things were bleak, though, as Michigan held a 20-6 advantage at halftime.

As the snow thickened, the Wolverines' attack intensified. In the third quarter, Jack Weisenburger broke free on a 22-yard scoring run. A little more than a minute separated Michigan's final two scoring runs in the fourth.

The Badgers had entered the contest with a respectable defense – one that had already notched a pair of shutouts. But Wilson and Bob Weiske, dubbed the "twins of destruction," had a difficult time slowing down the Michigan rushing attack. Chappuis, Elliot and Weisenburger all gained 75 or more yards in the contest, each of them having averaged better than five yards per carry.

And when Michigan needed to pass, Chappuis and Elliot always had someone to throw to.

Says Wilson, "They had scouted us well and took advantage of some things our defense was not prepared to handle. They ran a single wing offense. When they needed a few yards, it seemed it always ended up being the same player who was wide open behind their end and flanker in the flat. We didn't have a defense that could stop that play."

When Wisconsin had the ball, Michigan had little trouble slowing down Stuhldreher's open-huddle offense.

"It was obvious they were familiar with our play-calling," says Wilson. "To explain it in a simplified fashion: The play was three sets of digits. For example, the first might be 22, then 45, the third 33 and then hike. Michigan knew what our system was. I don't have any doubt this was the case. When the play was called, the second digit of the first number indicated the direction our play was to go. I can recall as the center, if the play was an even number, the play would go to the right and the player in front of me would take off to his left – the direction of our play – immediately as the ball was snapped."

"So their defense was made to look much better that day than it otherwise would have. At any rate, we got shellacked."

Wilson and his teammates tried to convince Stuhldreher of this but the coach was hesitant to believe it. "It wasn't until late in the game that he finally conceded," says Wilson. "By that time we were out of contention."

In the end, the 40-6 defeat had been every bit as miserable as the team's loss to California earlier that season. "It had been a gloomy day," says Wilson, "and our showing was nothing to rave about."

Crisler called it the best performance his players had given all year, but then added "... that Wilson sure is a honey" - his way of showing respect for how well Wisconsin's star had performed on both sides of the ball.

"We made some costly mistakes and you can't do that against a team like Michigan," Stuhldreher told reporters.

The Badgers weren't alone; no team fared well against the Maize and Blue that season. Crisler's team shut out Ohio State, then blanked USC, 49-0, in the Rose Bowl to claim the national championship.

>>>

Devastated by the Michigan loss, the Badgers travelled the following week to Minnesota where they lost, 21-0.

"During my playing days we never did beat Minnesota," says Wilson. "They had a good team, but some very large people. Two of their linemen were in the 260-pound range, which was very large in those days. I think the heaviest player we had was 220. So their man-power was greater than ours."

It was an ugly end to what had been one of the program's best seasons in years.

The 1948 season was Stuhldreher's last on the sidelines. The Badgers opened with a 1-2 mark before hosting Yale at Camp Randall. "Based on the 'Goodbye, Harry' chants that game it was obvious people were not happy with how things were going," says Wilson. Wisconsin was shut out by Minnesota for a third straight year and won just two games that entire season.

Then Ivy Williamson took over the program and change was noticeable as early as the 1949 season opener against Marquette. "We lined up for a field goal and instead of kicking it we ran the ball and scored a touchdown," says Wilson. "That play brought the people out of their seats because it was something we would have never done under Harry. That '49 team was kind of a renaissance for the Wisconsin program."

For all his efforts, Wilson was twice selected first-team all-conference (1947 and 1949) and is the only player in Badgers football history to be named the team's most valuable player three years in a row.

After concluding his career on the gridiron, Wilson faced a very difficult decision, as he had been invited to play both professional baseball and football. The Cleveland Browns selected Wilson in the fourth round of the 1950 Draft – the 52nd player selected overall.

Nagging shoulder and hand injuries pushed Wilson toward

baseball. "Even though I had a good football career, I just didn't think I could hold up."

After Wisconsin finished up at the College World Series in Omaha, Nebraska, Wilson signed a contract with the Chicago White Sox, for whom he played in the minor leagues until he was traded to Detroit. His best season at the plate during his Big League career was arguably 1956, when he batted .289, hit seven home runs and drove in 38 runs for the Tigers. After having raced around on the same fields as Satchel Paige, Warren Spahn and Stan Musial, Wilson's baseball career ended in 1960.

"It's difficult to say whether one has made a good decision or a bad decision," says Wilson, "but I am so relieved at this point of my life that I didn't play football simply by looking at some of my peers who did and have trouble getting around these days."

"And baseball has provided a much better retirement program than a career in football would have."

Wilson spent the next few years of his life testing out jobs – first insurance, then working at a clothing store – before he was asked to accept a position at a Madison-area bank which later became part of the M&I branch. Wilson kept that position for 30 years until his retirement.

Today he volunteers his time to help people grow their small businesses and plays tennis and golf.

PAT O'DONAHUE
1949-1951

The nuns of Eau Claire's St. Patrick's High School all expected better from young Pat O'Donahue. Good Catholic boys are supposed to attend Notre Dame, not Wisconsin. But O'Donahue didn't fashion himself a good Catholic boy – just a kid wanting to play college football, and Notre Dame wasn't much interested.

A local attorney had written to Notre Dame coach Frank Leahy about O'Donahue, a dominating force for the school of just 275 students. Leahy took the bait and attended St. Pat's annual football banquet.

"I was just a skinny, scrawny guy," recalls O'Donahue. "The lawyer took me up to the table to introduce me and I'll never forget, Leahy put his hand out and we shook hands and he said, 'Son, how big are you?' I lied to him, said 6-1 and 200 pounds. He just turned his head away and that's the last I heard from him. Never said a word to me."

Later, Leahy wrote to the O'Donahue family suggesting that if Pat were willing to work hard in the classroom and on the football field for his first two years in South Bend, Leahy would put him on scholarship for his last two. "My dad couldn't afford a ticket across the Eau Claire River," laughs O'Donahue, "so we crossed Notre Dame off our list."

Desperate to keep one of its top prospects at home, the

University of Wisconsin dispatched one of its assistant coaches immediately.

"George Lanphear came to my house and finally just pounded on the table and said to my dad, 'Mr. O'Donahue this is what I'm offering you, and Pat you better listen. I want your son at Wisconsin and it's never going to cost you one penny out of your pocket.'"

"I was kind of a smart ass, so I said 'Are you going to put that in writing?' and he said 'Yes, I will.'"

And so it was, Pat O'Donahue was going to be a Badger. The news didn't sit well with the folks at St. Pat's.

"I was ostracized right from the moment I did that. The nuns disowned me, the priest disowned me. (In their minds) I was going to an atheistic school which went against all of their preachings and teachings. I was beginning to wonder if I was going to get a diploma from their school. Father Paul came down the next day when the news had broken. I was mowing the lawn and he pulled up front in his car and he just rolled the window down and stared and then said, 'Be a good boy' and, vroom, he was gone."

O'Donahue was invited to play in the North-South High School All-Star Game where he made fast friends with guys like Eugene Felker and Jim Hammond – both of whom would later join him at Madison. "We had all decided to go to Wisconsin and bail them out," laughs O'Donahue. "Back in 1947 and '48 things weren't too good, and I'll be damned if all of those guys with scholarship offers to other places didn't end up in Madison. It was not a braggadocious place to go. They couldn't win diddley."

Things in Madison changed quickly.

After waiting out their first season (freshmen were not eligible to participate in those years), a number of the players from that class found their way into the lineup as sophomores in 1949 – the same year Ivy Williamson took over as coach of the program.

"Ivy came in as this young guy from out East, full of piss and vinegar, and was a great coach. He never had a losing season in (my) three years, which was nice because Wisconsin had come off a number of losing seasons. They were good seasons, they were learning seasons for us young guys. We got our heads bashed in and learned the hard way. It made us the big busters around campus and we got fat heads over it, but it was a lot of fun."

The men enjoyed campus life, as well. In those days, says O'Donahue, it was all "good, clean fun."

O'Donahue and his Madison buddies could play football, too.

During one stretch in the 1949 and 1950 seasons, Wisconsin won eight of 10 games, including a 14-13 victory over a top 10-ranked Northwestern squad. Williamson's six wins in 1950 had been the most since the team's legendary 1942 season, and that year the Badgers ended a four-year drought against rival Minnesota.

But Williamson's best season still lay ahead.

GAME I WON'T FORGET
October 6, 1951
at Illinois

In 1951, the Big Ten that fans know today had yet to be born. Woody Hayes was beginning his first season in Columbus, and the rivalry between his Buckeyes and the University of Michigan had yet to fully take shape. The media favored two teams to clash for the Big 10 title – Illinois and Wisconsin, a team that had dealt the Illini a loss the year before.

"Illinois was the big rooster in those days," says O'Donahue. "It wasn't so much Ohio State or Michigan, it was Illinois. We knew we had a ballclub that could beat them, and we went after them."

In that 1950 contest, O'Donahue acknowledges the 15th ranked Illini outperformed Wisconsin in just about every category except for where it counted most. Illinois had twice as many first downs and collected 242 yards to Wisconsin's 92. Still, the Badgers claimed the 7-6 victory.

Due to a scheduling agreement between the schools, O'Donahue and the Badgers would have to head back to Memorial Stadium for a third straight year. "We were like natural born citizens of Illinois," he jokes. "We didn't appreciate it much, and never had the advantage of a home field."

After Wisconsin knocked off Marquette 22-6 to open the season, word was getting around that the Badger defense was one of the best in the country. Dubbed Hard Rocks, O'Donahue was part of a front line that included Felker at the other end, Jerry Smith, Bob Leu and Bob Kennedy in the interior, Hal Faverty, Deral Teteak and Roger Dornburg at linebacker, and Ed Withers, Hammond and Billy Lane in the secondary. After missing action against Marquette, Felker and Teteak returned for the contest against the Illini, bringing the Badgers back to almost full strength.

It was a defense without a weak link, and O'Donahue was its leader.

Wrote Henry J. McCormick of the *Wisconsin State Journal* a couple of days before kickoff, "If there is a better defensive end in college football than Patrick J. O'Donahue, he has escaped my attention. He is the ringleader of a defensive platoon that is rugged enough to harry the best attack."

But even with that defense, oddsmakers had made Illinois a six-point favorite after seeing Ray Eliot's Illini trounce UCLA 27-13 in the season opener, much thanks to star running back Johnny Karras' three touchdowns.

Billed as the Illini offense against the Badger defense, even the UW coaching staff was buying into how good Illinois' rushing attack was – at least when speaking to reporters. Said Williamson, "We sort of expect Illinois to score, but we hope to score enough times to come out on top."

Ultimately, however, it was Wisconsin's lack of offense that proved to be the difference-maker in O'Donahue's last crack at the Illini.

The start of the game was pushed back an hour to accommodate Game 3 of the 1951 World Series between the Yankees and Giants. The 56,207 fans in the stadium and coast-to-coast television audience watched Illinois score first. Karras capped a 72-yard drive with a six-yard touchdown run.

The Badgers scored their only touchdown later in the first half when a botched handoff from Karras to Don Stevens resulted in a fumble; Hammond pounced on the ball in the end zone. A field goal gave Wisconsin a 10-7 halftime lead.

Throughout the game a total of four players were ejected for unnecessary roughness, two from each team. The biggest loss may have been Withers, the Badgers' outstanding defensive back who was said to have been provoked by Illinois receiver Joe Vernasco during an on-field fight. Wisconsin also lost Smith to a side scuffle.

The turning point in the game occurred in the second half. With Wisconsin still holding its three-point lead, the Badgers had a first-and-goal from the one-yard line but the drive was killed by failed rushing attempts and penalties. On one play, a controversial pre-snap illegal motion call cost the Badgers dearly.

"They said we had a guard pulling too soon," says O'Donahue. "I remember standing there listening to the official. The play didn't call for the guard to pull. Nobody could figure out what the hell this guy was talking about. The man in motion was called to go in motion, and did so legally. We never did score."

After taking over on downs, the Illini launched an offensive attack that took them deep into Wisconsin territory. The game's pivotal play proved to be a desperation third-and-19 pass from Don Engels that bounced off the hands of Illinois end Steve Nosek and into the arms of teammate Rex Smith, who was downed at the eight-yard line. Two plays later Karras plunged into the end zone for the second time that afternoon to give Illinois a 14-10 lead.

The Badgers charged again on the arm of John Coatta, but came up short; Coatta's pass to Harland Carl in the end zone was batted down to help secure the victory for Illinois.

Wrote McCormick in the *State Journal's* Monday edition, "Illinois had the punch when it was vital, and Wisconsin didn't."

It had been the opposite result of the year before. The Badgers out-gained Illinois 110 yards to 29 on the ground, and collected 20 first downs to Illinois' eight. But Williamson put the statistics in perspective following the loss. "It's the points that count," he told a reporter, "not the first downs."

"It's been a nothing spot in my mind for a long time," says O'Donahue. "It was a game we deserved to win, and we had earned it. We had the ball all afternoon and couldn't score. We were inside the 10 and five-yard line (many) times and didn't score. You do that and you're not going to win many games."

As well as he played, and as successful a season as Wisconsin had in 1951, that loss still burns O'Donahue to this day.

"I guess people say 'forget it, it's over with,'" he says. "I've tried. I just can't."

>>>

After Illinois, the road didn't get any easier for O'Donahue and his Hard Rocks pals. Ohio State had lost to Michigan State that same weekend and was hungry for victory in its trip to Madison. As their coach's wife, Anne Hayes, put it, "Gosh! I'd hate to be Wisconsin next Saturday. Woody's kinda mad."

Reeling from its loss, it was up to O'Donahue and the team's other seniors to refocus.

"Ivan encouraged us to have meetings ourselves and get things ironed out. He didn't want no temperaments flying around, no finger pointing. We decided that the reason we came to Wisconsin was to pull them out of the doldrums, so we decided we'd do what we could to get back on the winning streak. We knew we were damn good football players. We just had to get off our dead ass."

The Badgers played the Buckeyes to a 6-6 tie, and then allowed a total of just 27 points in the final six contests to post a 7-1-1 record. By the end of the year it was clear Wisconsin owned the best defense in the country and was worthy of its top 10 ranking. The 16-7 win over Penn was especially satisfying; the year before Penn had beaten up Wisconsin physically in a 20-0 shutout. All year long the Badgers had waited to get even. "We had made a pledge and we kept it. We pounded them into the ground fast and furious ... They were the big shots and we put them in the corner whimpering." That game, says O'Donahue, started a feud that lasts until this day. "They broke off relations before they left the field that afternoon. You can count the years. They have not made up relations yet."

But only one Big Ten team got to go to a bowl in 1951, and thanks to its 27 fourth quarter points, 9-0-1 Illinois was able to claim its second Rose Bowl victory under Eliot.

"We had no power over it. It was over with," says O'Donahue. "7-1-1 is not a bad record, but it came down to that Illinois game."

If still sore over how things turned out that season, O'Donahue remains a loyal member of the Hard Rocks defense he was a part of. It was one of the finest group of defenders ever assembled in the Big Ten, he believes.

"We had probably one of the best groups that ever stayed together, lived together and played together," he says. "We all graduated and all got our diploma, and I don't know of any of us that failed in business or coaching or anything else. We were a bunch of renegades but we all turned out alright."

"There wasn't a piker on our ball club, I'll tell you that."

Joined by fellow Hard Rocks teammate Jerry Smith, O'Donahue spent a season in San Francisco playing pro football for coach Buck Shaw. He returned a punt for a touchdown and made his lone extra point attempt. "Had a great time out in San Francisco, a great season," he says. "But Uncle Sam took care of my future."

O'Donahue was five credits short of his degree when he left Wisconsin. As long as he was working toward it, the army would leave him be. But with one game remaining in the 1952 NFL season they came calling. "They let me play that game, then they took me into the army and shipped me off to Japan for 16 months."

When he returned, O'Donahue was traded to Green Bay, where he says coach Lisle Blackbourn was unhappy to see him. Blackbourn had been an assistant at Wisconsin when O'Donahue first arrived on campus, and had coached at Marquette for the remainder of O'Donahue's collegiate career.

"In terms of Xs and Os, Lisle took a back seat to nobody, even Paul Brown," says O'Donahue. "But he just couldn't handle any kid over the age of 18.

"I decided there had to be life after football, so I hung 'em up."

In the years since, O'Donahue has remained a strong supporter of Badger football, doing whatever he can to promote the program. He's kept his memories of those Hard Rocks years, and his sense of humor. Shares O'Donahue about his recent cataract surgery, "I had seven concussions playing ball and I figured if they froze my head it might crack."

DALE HACKBART
1957-1959

O n pass play after pass play, Dale Hackbart sprinted down the field and caught the football with ease, then turned and fired it back to the center. This repeated for a few days at the start of the 1952 football season before, finally, Madison East's freshman coach pulled the ninth grader aside. Hackbart had signed up to play end but Claude Hungerford had another position in mind. Hungerford had Hackbart take a few snaps from under center, then convinced his new star that he was a better fit at quarterback.

"That was the beginning of my career," says Hackbart.

Hackbart starred for the freshman squad, then for junior varsity, and as a senior was one of the top offensive players in the Big 8 Conference. "I was selected the all-city quarterback, then the all-area quarterback, then the all-state quarterback," he says.

By this point, University of Wisconsin coach Milt Bruhn was making regular contact with the local prep standout. But things came to a screeching halt, says Hackbart, after an incident his senior year of basketball. A large number of the varsity team's players clashed with the basketball coach over who deserved to be in the lineup; ultimately, Hackbart and a few friends were kicked off the team.

Says Hackbart, "We were young, and dumb, and not paying attention. You know how young guys are? I think at the time, Milt

Bruhn and the University of Wisconsin thought that maybe I was a bad kid with a bad attitude."

Hackbart started to entertain the idea of going to Minnesota instead, but a hangup with the enrollment office eliminated the Gophers as an option. Two days after he got the bad news from Minnesota he took a call from Bruhn; Hackbart was instructed to meet the coach at his office immediately.

"He told me that he wouldn't let me out of his office until I signed with the University of Wisconsin," laughs Hackbart. "Which I did."

Having grown up on Madison's east side, where his father owned a barber shop within a stone's throw from the Oscar Mayer plant, Hackbart had snuck into Badger football games as a kid. Now he was on the fast track to being one of the team's main attractions.

At first, playing wasn't as much of an obstacle as remaining academically eligible. Hackbart admits he was a D-student when he arrived, mostly because he had yet to learn how to properly study. Bruhn set him up with a tutor and after that he cruised in the classroom.

Toward the end of the 1957 season, Bruhn went with his sophomore passer in games against Northwestern, Illinois and Minnesota. The Badgers won all three contests, and Hackbart won the starting quarterback job, which he kept for the remainder of his career.

At the start of the 1958 season, Hackbart and his teammates rattled off another three wins, then lost to Iowa before a trip to Columbus. The Badgers hadn't beaten the Buckeyes since 1946, but they were confident it was a streak that would end, even on the road.

With the game on the line, Wisconsin was faced with third down and goal at the one-yard line, but Badger running backs Billy Hobbs and Ron Steiner got stopped on consecutive downs and the game ended with a 7-7 tie.

Says Hackbart, who scored Wisconsin's only points on a punt return, "When you look at the film, clearly both of our backs went over the pile and got pushed back and the officials didn't give us a touchdown. Had we beaten Ohio State we would have gone to the Rose Bowl, even though we had lost to Iowa. Milt Bruhn was just irate (with the officiating)."

It was a bitter pill to swallow for the 7-1-1 club ... it was also motivation for the following year.

GAME I WON'T FORGET
October 24, 1959
vs Ohio State

To start the 1959 season, the Badgers beat a highly-touted Miami-Florida team and collected a pair of home victories over Stanford and Marquette before making the trip to West Lafayette, Indiana. Purdue hadn't been much of a challenge for Hackbart the year before, but this wasn't the same Boilermakers team, and the Badgers didn't play the same game as they had in their 31-6 victory in 1958. On a field of mud, Purdue won, 21-0. "We made a lot of mistakes, fumbled the ball – just didn't play well. Following that, Milt got out and worked the hell out of us and said that if we were going to win the Big Ten, we've got to start with Iowa."

The Hawkeyes had given Wisconsin its only loss the year before – a 20-9 pounding – and waltzed into Camp Randall with the No. 9 ranking in the country. The Badgers punched their way to a 25-0 lead early in the second half, but Iowa didn't die without a fight. "It was a grudge match, to a certain degree," says Hackbart. "We got off to a great start ... But they came back toward the end of the game and it was nip and tuck." Wisconsin won, 25-16.

Now another 'grudge match' was on the horizon.

"Milt reminded us during the week that we had been robbed in Columbus. Milt just said, 'We're going to line up and it's going to be smash mouth football,' and that's basically what it was."

There was talk in the papers leading up to the game that Hackbart and the offense might try a little trickery. "(Offensive coordinator) Perry Moss' trick play was to put me back in the spread ... we never did. Perry was always coming up with ideas like that, but we never got to a point where we were ahead and could use something like that."

What did prove successful against Woody Hayes' Buckeye squad was misdirection. "When we ran Bob Zeman in motion, nine times out of 10 we'd run that way," says Hackbart. "We put a play in where the halfback would take a half-step in that direction, then run a counter. That was effective against Ohio State."

The game was played on a torn-up field, and in winds that affected both teams' kicking and passing games. The winner of the contest would be the one that controlled the action up front;

fortunately the Badgers had Dan Lanphear ... and Ohio State did not.

Not only did Lanphear help to slow the Buckeyes backfield of Bob White, Bob Ferguson and quarterback Tom Matte, but just four minutes into the game he blocked a punt which rolled out of the end zone to give the Badgers a 2-0 lead. A short while later, a seven-yard Hackbart run made it 9-0. "Milt told me to run the pass-run option to the right. After I got outside the tackles I could see there was an opening. I just barreled into the end zone. That's when everybody got excited."

Wisconsin kickers Jim Bakken and Karl Holzwarth each missed field goals in the half, but thanks to a pass interference call against Ohio State, Holzwarth got a second opportunity, making the score 12-3 at halftime.

Any hope Ohio State had of climbing back into the game was washed away on a third quarter possession. After a Wisconsin fumble gave Ohio State the football at the Wisconsin 13-yard line, the Buckeyes failed to make much ground on first and second down. "Then Lanphear really popped one of their backs and they fumbled. That probably saved us."

On another possession, Hackbart chased down Ferguson, who had a clear path to the end zone. "I tackled him in front of the bench and our players were all going nuts," says Hackbart. "They didn't score on that series. I know for a fact that had I not made the tackle he would have scored."

Ohio State also had a 27-yard touchdown pass negated due to an illegal motion penalty.

All of those missed opportunities infuriated Hayes. And nothing made the Badger players more delighted than to see Woody unnerved. "If you got near him, or if you made a tackle near their sideline, Woody was always in your face, yelling at you," laughs Hackbart. "That's just the way he coached. And it didn't make any difference if it was nine-below or 90, he was out there with that hat and short-sleeve shirt."

Neither team scored a single point in the second half, preserving Wisconsin's 12-3 win. The Badgers out-gained the Buckeyes 235 to 168 on the ground and committed fewer turnovers – the formula for a winning day in rough conditions.

Hayes agreed. "Milt Bruhn is a fine football coach, and he deserved to win this one," Ohio State's coach said afterward. "I'm not saying I want Wisconsin to win the championship, but I do say it couldn't happen to a finer bunch of players and coaches. We just got beat by a better team."

>>>

The next two weeks, Hackbart helped his team to beat Michigan and No. 2 ranked Northwestern on the road. Then the team ran into trouble at home against Illinois.

"We were up on Illinois, with time running out in the fourth quarter, and they had to go 60 or 70 yards to score a touchdown with no timeouts left," recalls Hackbart. "The Badger fans were making so much noise and yelling so loud that the officials kept stopping the game and Illinois was able to regroup. They went right down and scored on us."

But a win over Minnesota and a Northwestern loss gave Bruhn's club the title and the opportunity to go to Pasadena. It had been a long and tiring season. "When you look at what the Big Ten was in the late 1950s and early 1960s, with the exception of Indiana, any of those Big Ten teams could go to the Rose Bowl," says Hackbart.

Tired or not, Bruhn was not about to let his team rest in their preparation for the biggest game of the year. The Badgers arrived in California two weeks early, and Bruhn had the club on a two-a-day schedule from the moment they got there.

"They practiced the hell out of us," says Hackbart. "It was just like 'Give us a break. You don't have to worry about us. Just let us get our legs back.'"

Says Hackbart, "About three days before the game, we all got on the bus after practice. During that session guys were fighting with each other. They were tired. They were angry. It's like we had all erupted. The coaches were trying to break up this fight, break up that fight – it was just frustration from being out there."

"This story has really never been told," Hackbart continues. "We got on the bus to head back to the hotel and the seniors got together, and some of the juniors, and decided that we didn't want to play the game. Bob Zeman and Jerry Stalcup, our two captains, stopped Milt when he got on the bus and they said, 'Milt, we're tired. We've been beating each other up.' And basically they said, 'We want to go home. We don't want to play this game.'"

"I think it absolutely devastated Milt."

The Badgers coaching staff had been accusing the players of partying too much that week and not focusing on the game, but Hackbart says that was never the case. "Mike Stankey had a big room and we'd fill his bath tub with beer and order sandwiches from the catering service and sit in drinking beer and eating sandwiches. Nobody was going out. We were too damn tired to go out.

But somehow or another Milt had got that impression."

The Badgers stayed in Pasadena to play the game, but lost soundly to Washington, 44-8.

"It's not that we didn't go out there and play our best," says Hackbart. "We didn't lay down. I just think that whole week was an emotional stress. It just was not our best football game."

"The only guys I've ever spoken to about this were my teammates, and we all feel bad about it. I know it was extremely hard and tough on Milt."

After Hackbart finished up his Madison career with an impressive 17-4-1 record as a starter, he played minor league baseball briefly for the Pittsburgh Pirates organization before joining the Green Bay Packers.

Green Bay was already plenty deep at quarterback in 1960, so coach Vince Lombardi tabbed Hackbart to play in the secondary. "I was competing with Willie Wood and Emlen Tunnell, and Emlen had been with Lombardi when he was in New York. He was getting on in age but he was still a hell of a player, and one of us had to go." Ultimately, it was Hackbart, who was traded to the Redskins.

In his first season in Washington, Hackbart collected six interceptions, including two he returned for touchdowns. Hackbart finished his career in 1973 at the age of 35. Just prior to that he and former Badger teammate Jim Holmes started a tire business in Colorado. Since 1983, Hackbart has worked for the Bridgestone/Firestone Company as an outside salesman – a job he has continued into his 70s.

"I don't get up in the morning and say, 'Damn, I've got to go to work.' I enjoy the challenge," he says.

PAT RICHTER
1960-1962

What Vince Lombardi didn't know wasn't going to hurt him. At least that's how Pat Richter saw it. So when the NFL receiver and punter was asked to take a little big-league batting practice, Richter pushed the policies of the Washington Redskins' head coach to the back of his mind. After all, it's not every day one gets to hit for the great Ted Williams.

"The Washington Senators had a batting practice catcher named George Susce who had been with the Milwaukee Braves when I worked out with them (as a high school prospect in 1958)," says Richter. "One day I bumped into him and he said, 'Hey come on down, I want to have Ted see you hit.'"

Richter hadn't swung a bat in years but was excited to step into the box and take a few pitches from Senators assistant coach Don Zimmer. "I knew Lombardi would kill me if he found out, but I snuck down there and took some batting practice – hit a few line drives, hit a few outs – and after that we went over and talked to Williams. For 15 minutes we talked. It was just fascinating. He asked stuff like 'Where were your hands when you hit the ball?' or 'How did your hips move?'"

Years later, Richter traded memories with Zimmer when the Major League Baseball All-Star Game came to Milwaukee. "Even though it had been 30 years since we had seen each other it seemed like it had been yesterday."

The memory is one of Richter's fondest, and had a few things gone differently during his stay at the University of Wisconsin, it's possible the Madison native would have been playing for Williams every day instead of for Lombardi.

Born in 1941, Richter grew up on the city's east side where he and his buddies challenged the neighborhood's older kids on a patch of grass that bordered on Lake Monona. "In baseball, you had to learn how to hit the ball up the middle," says Richter. "If you hit it one way it'd go into the houses and the other way it'd go into the lake, and it'd be your responsibility to go get it." When they had to, they snuck into Lakewood Grade School in Maple Bluff to play basketball. Every afternoon there was something to play.

By high school Richter stood out in football, basketball and baseball for Madison East. He joined Bill Raftery on *Parade Magazine*'s All-American basketball squad. One of the local scouts for the Braves got him the tryout at County Stadium. "Went down with my parents, went to the ballgame and dressed up in a Braves uniform. All the guys were there – Aaron, Mathews and Adcock. What a thrill!"

Football wasn't a priority when he was considering where to attend college, even though he had served as his school's tight end his final two seasons. Richter was focused on basketball, and if it were possible, would try to play baseball as well. Letters poured in from all over, giving Richter plenty of options.

"I originally signed to go to Kansas to play basketball. I look back on it today and it's crazy because I never saw Phog Allen Fieldhouse and I still signed the tender."

When Richter returned to Madison, his advisor, Gene Calhoun, rerouted the prep phenom. "He said if I was interested in baseball that I'd be better off in the Big Ten. So I changed my mind and accepted the basketball scholarship from Wisconsin instead."

By August of 1959, however, Richter was starting to get the itch to play football again. Afraid of what Wisconsin's basketball coach might say, the freshman had one of the assistant football coaches ask for him. "They did the dirty work and I got to go out for the freshman football team."

After basketball season there was no freshman baseball, so Richter participated in spring football. By fall he was in a regular routine, with no time in between seasons for a break.

"It's so much different today than back then," says Richter. "We didn't even have a weight program. It was as simple as, from 2 p.m. to 6 p.m. I knew I wasn't going to be studying, so it was natural for me to play sports and manage my studying at another time."

As a sophomore in 1960, Richter quickly became the Badgers' top target in the passing game. "Ron Miller was the quarterback at that time and our first game was against Stanford. I think I caught six or seven passes, which was more than anyone had caught up to that point. Then in the fifth game against Michigan I caught a long pass - the longest of my short season - and as I was being tackled the defender grabbed both of my arms and pulled me down and I broke my collarbone and was out for the rest of the season."

A little less than two months later Richter was back at it - first basketball, then baseball. But by the time the fall rolled around football was no longer just an offseason activity to keep the 228-pound Richter occupied; he had become Milt Bruhn's star playmaker, and football had become his top priority.

GAME I WON'T FORGET
November 25, 1961
at Minnesota

With Miller and Richter back for the 1961 season, Bruhn had some blocks with which to start building a winner. But the club faced three top 10-ranked opponents in the season's first six games and each did a number on Wisconsin: Michigan State (20-0), Iowa (47-15) and Ohio State (30-21).

After a pair of victories over Northwestern and Illinois, all that was left for 5-3 Wisconsin was the season finale against a Minnesota squad that had finished the previous season with the top national ranking in both the AP and UPI polls.

"It had become the traditional end-of-the-season game. Now we play for the Axe, but it wasn't in front of us back then. It existed but it wasn't something you ran across the field to grab if you won the game. It's more high energy today. Still, it was an intense rivalry that had built up over the years. (Minnesota coach) Murray Warmath and Milt went way back, so it was a coaching rivalry as well. Milt had graduated from Minnesota and had been a star during his time there."

The Buckeyes and Gophers were dueling it out for the conference title heading into that last weekend, neither team having had to play the other. The Gophers' only loss came in the season opener against Missouri. They rattled off six Big Ten wins before the Wisconsin game, although four of those wins had come by a margin of seven or fewer points.

"We went into that last game against Minnesota with nothing on the line," says Richter. "They had a nice team with Sandy Stephens, Bobby Bell, Tom Hall. Our discussions heading into that game centered around the idea that let's knock them off, scuff 'em up a bit ... put a blemish on their season."

An estimated 10,000 Badgers fans made their way across the Mississippi for the most important contest of their team's season. The snow that flattened Minnesota that week didn't affect the playing conditions at Memorial Stadium. The University had put a tarp on the field with air blowing underneath it. By game time the grass was perfect for a November battle.

The beginning of the game, however, was anything but perfect for Wisconsin. After a long kick return, Wisconsin was forced to settle for a 38-yard field goal, only to watch it go awry. On the Gophers' first play from scrimmage, Stephens hit Hall on a quick strike that went for a touchdown. Recalls Richter, "If you watch the film you can see Tom Hall waving his hands to the quarterback because we only had 10 men on the field. Somebody had forgotten to go out there and nobody was covering the receiver. So Stephens just turned and popped the ball and he went 80 yards for a touchdown to start the game. After that, as the game went on, things started to go our way."

The Gophers' top-rated defense immediately had trouble with Wisconsin's passing attack. Late in the first quarter Miller hit Richter for a 40-yard score to tie the game, and on almost all of their first half possessions the Badgers advanced the ball at will on Minnesota. The problem for Wisconsin wasn't advancing, it was finishing; the team's senior kicker, Jim Bakken, missed all four of his first-half field goal attempts (a bad snap on a fifth field goal killed yet another drive deep in Minnesota territory).

In the third quarter, Bakken missed another field goal, this one hitting the crossbar from 46 yards out. Fortunately, the defense stepped forward to help. Jim Nettles gave the Badgers a 14-7 lead by returning a Stephens interception 60 yards for a score. The No. 3-ranked Gophers regained the lead briefly, thanks to a fumble recovery that led to a 22-yard Jerry Jones touchdown run and two-point conversion. But Wisconsin answered back, this time with Richter making a circus catch to put Wisconsin ahead 20-15.

The Badgers had a chance to put away Warmath's club late in the game. With a first and goal at the six-yard line, the Badgers failed to drive the ball in, instead losing seven yards. In his only successful try of the afternoon, Bakken made his sixth (and most important) attempt to pad the Wisconsin lead to eight.

In the final minutes the Gophers marched down the field one last time. Stephens hit Jim Cairns for an important gain before finding Al Fischer in the end zone. But the two-point attempt failed when Bakken, of all people, knocked down the pass to save the 23-21 win for Wisconsin.

Miller completed 19 of 37 passes in the victory for 297 yards, almost half of which went to Richter (142 yards, two scores).

Because Ohio State beat Michigan, 50-20, the Gophers were nudged out of the Big Ten top spot by Wisconsin. Ohio State declined the Rose Bowl invite, however, allowing Minnesota to travel to Pasadena where they soundly rolled UCLA, 21-3.

In Richter's mind, the win over the Gophers was the catalyst for Wisconsin's remarkable Rose Bowl season of 1962.

"There was great leadership on that team, great camaraderie ... and that game brought everything together. It gave us a good boost into spring and then fall the next season."

The 1961 season also gave Richter a little notoriety; his 47 receptions that year broke Jerry Witt's UW career mark of 46, and his 817 yards set a new single-season record and helped him to eclipse Dave Schreiner's career total. Richter also set new career totals for catches and receiving yards in the conference.

"We really didn't keep track of that sort of stuff because we had a mediocre record," says Richter, "but it did bring some recognition and helped get All-American status."

>>>

After the football season wrapped up, Richter and the rest of the Badgers hoops squad surprised a Jerry Lucas – and John Havlicek – led Ohio State team that was riding a 47-game winning streak and later made it to the NCAA final. Richter played mostly as a reserve for the team, earning his court time by grabbing rebounds. "Even though I was on scholarship, basketball was the sport in which I had the least success. It was enjoyable but it ended up being a transitional sport."

The Badger baseball squad knocked off the University of Michigan that year in a season-ending double header to push the Wolverines out of the conference lead. In the second game, Richter was at the plate with two outs, one man on base and his team trailing by a run. "You couldn't have scripted it any better," he says. Michigan made a pitching change, bringing in Fritz Fischer, who threw just one pitch. "It looked like a balloon, I just crushed it. It started about four feet high and by the time it got over the fence it was about six feet high – just a dart." Michigan later went on to win the College World Series.

"As an athlete, it was a special year for me," says Richter.

Personally, it took a toll. Richter's father passed away not long after the football season had ended. "It changed my personal circumstances and I started to wonder about going to play professional baseball," he says. Prior to that, Richter had only been on a partial need-based scholarship due to his family's income level. After his father died Richter qualified to receive a full scholarship his final year.

In 1962, Richter and his teammates strolled to an 8-1 record and the Big Ten title. In the Rose Bowl loss to USC, Richter set a record with 11 catches for 163 yards. Unfortunately, the Badgers' passing game ran out of time in the 42-37 defeat.

Though pro baseball would have been happy to have him, Richter had made up his mind on football. He had spent a summer playing baseball in the Basin League in South Dakota for $320 a month. "Our first game of my senior season was a triple header, about 33 degrees, a little snow on the ground. The game on Friday was postponed so we played a nine-inning and two seven-inning games on Saturday beginning at 8 o'clock in the morning. That soured me a bit on the game. And baseball had a more extensive minor league system, whereas in professional football you're either at the top or you're going on with the rest of your life. It's very definitive."

In an August all-star exhibition pitting college football's finest against the NFL's best team, Richter and his teammates beat the Packers at Soldiers Field, 20-17. That college team was hardly a group of amateurs, featuring future Hall of Famers Bobby Bell, Buck Buchanan and John Mackey, along with Richter and his senior season quarterback, Ron VanderKelen. "Ron and I hooked up for a 73-yard touchdown pass. Longest pass I ever caught."

The Washington Redskins nabbed Richter with the seventh overall selection in the 1963 NFL Draft – to this day he remains one of the highest drafted tight ends in league history. "Back then it was a lot of money, but today it doesn't seem like much. The bonus was $15,000 and the salary was $15,000 and escalated to $17,500 my second year," he says.

As a member of the Redskins, Richter got to rub elbows with some of the country's most famous and interesting people. "Washington was just a terrific town. We had connections with people in the FBI. Nixon would come to games and Bobby Kennedy was at practice. It was a fascinating place to be. But when you're 21, 22 you don't realize it."

Richter stayed in Washington for the bulk of his career, making a brief stop in Dallas before calling it quits in 1971.

"We didn't have very good records until Vince Lombardi came (in 1969). He just had a tremendous impact on you. He was running a hamburger drill one day in training camp and while making a block on a linebacker he inadvertently came up with his elbow above the protective facemask bar on my helmet and busted my nose. But the only thing going through my mind was to show Lombardi that I could take a little punishment. So I stayed in the drill. The next day I came in and started running and he hollered at me. He said, 'Take it easy.' He could push you to a breaking point, but then pull you back."

Richter earned his law degree from the University of Wisconsin. He had attended night school at American University while playing for the Redskins and attended classes at Madison in the spring. After he finished his career he briefly took a job at a Madison law firm before receiving an offer to work for Oscar Mayer in its human resources department.

While the UW athletic department and football program struggled throughout the 1980s, the university tried to recruit Richter's assistance more than once, but without success. "(Oscar Mayer) had treated us very well and I had a responsible position and didn't want to lose my family's privacy."

Then University of Wisconsin President Donna Shalala persuaded Richter to chair a strategic planning committee looking into why the football program was experiencing economic hardship. Richter's situation at Oscar Mayer was changing due to a merger with Kraft so when he and Shalala discussed the athletic director position again the timing was right.

"There was more accumulated debt there than was originally thought, and the facilities were in rough shape. And people from Wisconsin were down on the program. They didn't have any bragging rights," he says. "But things turned out well."

Quite well. Thanks in large part to Richter's leadership, Wisconsin's athletic programs are now on par with the school's academics – something that would have been incomprehensible to fans in 1989.

"I bump into people today and they say thank you, and I know what they mean. They now have those bragging rights and are proud of Badger athletics."

KEN BOWMAN
1961-1963

It's the kind of advice fathers commonly hand down to sons, but for whatever reason, for Ken Bowman the words stuck. "My father said, 'If you get good at some sport they'll give you a free ride to college. And that's probably the only way you'll get to college."

The Bowmans surely couldn't afford to send Ken to college on Oscar's wages. For years he had worked at International Harvester in Chicago, where, like clockwork, the company laid him off once it had built up a backlog of tractors and plows for the season. Nine months on, three months off – hardly enough to get by on. Eventually Oscar moved the family to the Quad Cities, where he started up a Standard Oil gas station. "It wasn't the business it is today," says Ken Bowman. "His margin was four cents a gallon. You had to pump a lot of gas to make any money."

Bowman hoped to have a better life and football became his tool to get there. "When I got to ninth grade I didn't know that much about organized football. The coach put me at fullback. Hell, I didn't know what a fullback did."

The next year, the area's four junior high squads pooled together at Rock Island High School. "There were four guys who had started previously at fullback, and the coach didn't have a center of any size or worth. He ran us in a race and I hate to admit it, but I finished last. So he made me the center."

And there Bowman stayed, helping his team in a stacked conference of bigger schools, such as Dubuque, Iowa City, Cedar Rapids and Davenport. "Heck, Davenport had one high school and they had 100,000 people. Rock Island had 40,000 people, so it was a little one sided."

Bowman "stretched out" in high school, growing to be 6-foot-3 and more than 200 pounds. He was a dominant force and was named all-state by the Chicago Daily News his senior year, edging out a highly-touted prospect at another Illinois prep school named Dick Butkus. Laughs Bowman, "I always say that he was a better defensive player, but I was a better center than he ever was."

Bowman no longer cared about having to play center. He was still focused on the real prize – the better life his father spoke of. "I had taken what my dad said to heart. I was going to get good at wherever they put me and get a free ride to college, no matter where it was. (My dad) was 51 when he passed. He worked himself to death to be a decent father and provide for his family. I wanted to get that education to make my life easier than what he had to go through."

Bowman visited the majority of the Big Ten schools and even paid a visit to Frank Kush at Arizona State. But a local businessman kept pushing Bowman toward Wisconsin, and arranged to drive the lineman to Madison for a basketball game and a visit with coach Milt Bruhn.

"Being from the south side of Chicago, I went up to Madison and thought I'd died and gone to heaven," says Bowman. "You walk along and look in Lake Mendota and can see the fish swimming. Just a pristine campus, just a beautiful place. And Milt was just a big ol' farmer it seemed to me; I don't think he had a dishonest bone in his body."

By the time freshman practice had finished Bowman had soured on Madison life. He was tired of practice without play, tired of being a whipping boy for the varsity. At one point he even convinced six of the other recruits to join Kush in sunny Arizona. But things cooled and fall soon arrived. Then Bowman became even more discontent. That year he was the backup to senior Dick Baer. The expectation was that Baer would get the lion's share of the snaps, but because players were still playing on both sides of the ball, Bowman would get plenty of time.

"My dad came up one Saturday for a game, because I had told him I would get time. Ron Henrice, another senior, was elevated to second string for the game. I was so mad I could spit. I told my dad, 'That's it. I'm done.' Frankly, I was embarrassed. My dad had to close down his gas station and drive up on a Saturday to see me sit on my butt." Oscar returned for the Badgers' next home game and jumped out of his seat when Ken was sent into the game. From that point on, Ken Bowman stopped looking for a way out of Madison.

The opportunity Bowman had sought at Madison academically also became an obstacle. Because of his poor grades in high school, the University would only let him enroll in physical education classes. "You took courses like swimming, badminton and basketball ... teaching courses. I really didn't like it, so I cut a deal with coach Bruhn that if I could get straight A's I would be let out of Phy. Ed. and be allowed into the school of Letters and Science. I didn't know what I wanted to do yet. I guess I wanted to be a football player, but we all know that doesn't last forever."

GAME I WON'T FORGET
January 1, 1963
vs Southern California

By the start of the 1962 season, Bowman was Bruhn's regular starting center, and next to tackle Roger Pillath and tight end Pat Richter he was one of the largest linemen on the roster. The quarterback position that year was up for grabs; Ron Miller, who had started the year before, had been denied a fifth year of eligibility. To replace him, Bruhn tracked down Ron VanderKelen, who had been on hiatus from the team. The coaching staff stayed on VanderKelen the entire camp, making sure he was both physically and mentally tested, and at times it almost broke the senior down. But he stuck it out, and as Bowman puts it, "did a whale of a job for us."

On the strength of the VanderKelen-to-Richter connection, the Badgers were an immediate threat to the Big Ten crown. The team won its first four games, then stumbled against Ohio State, 14-7. Bowman considers the loss a turning point.

"The Badgers didn't win in Columbus back then ... they don't win in Columbus today, it's tough," he says. "We got beat, but we only got beat by seven points. We thought if we can just about beat these guys, we can beat anybody."

Bowman was right; Wisconsin didn't lose another Big Ten contest, not even to top-ranked Northwestern. By the end of November the 8-1 Badgers were Rose Bowl bound. "I've been on some great teams," says Bowman, "and good teams just have a feeling. There's a never-quit attitude ... and we had that feeling that year."

What he and his teammates didn't have was a clue of what awaited them once they arrived in California a week before their anticipated matchup against No. 1-ranked USC. "They put us up in a monastery, can you believe that? Up in the mountains someplace. No lie. The first we came down from the mountain, as it were, was Friday before the Saturday game to practice in Pasadena," says Bowman.

"I always thought it was a mistake. There are a limited number of things to do at a monastery. We certainly didn't get put into a monastery when I was with the Packers prior to the Super Bowl, I can tell you that."

And if the conservative surroundings weren't a factor, Bowman believes the mental warfare waged by the local media certainly proved to be.

"Those folks down there did such a great job of pumping helium up our guys' hind ends," says Bowman. "Our tackle, Roger Pillath, was (later) the NCAA heavyweight champion. He was about 250 pounds, 6-foot-3, built ... and they were telling us they didn't have a chance against us. That we were too big for them. They had some of our guys believing all we had to do was walk out and throw our hats on the field and the game would be over."

"Unfortunately, it took us 30 minutes to figure out that wasn't the case."

The two teams traded touchdowns to start. USC scored first on a pass play from Pete Beathard to Ron Butcher, an offensive tackle who became an eligible receiver on the play; Wisconsin followed with a one-yard touchdown run. A pair of USC runs in the second quarter gave John McKay's Trojans a decided 21-7 lead at halftime.

"We were a little bit down, but again, good teams have that never-say-die attitude," says Bowman. "To beat a good team, you have to slug away for 60 minutes. We were a hell of a lot better than this. And our coaching staff started looking for weaknesses in their pass defense, and we started to get after Beathard."

But the rain kept pouring on Wisconsin. Beathard connected

with receiver Hal Bedsole for two scores in the third quarter, and after USC grabbed an interception Beathard threw his fourth touchdown two plays later to give USC a 42-14 lead at the start of the fourth quarter. McKay admitted afterward that his players began their celebration at that point, but the game was just beginning for Bowman and his offensive teammates.

Lou Holland scored on a 13-yard run to complete an 80-yard drive, then VanderKelen hit Gary Kroner from four yards out. The Badger passing attack could not be stopped by the USC defense, only the clock operator; at one point with four minutes remaining, a game official asked that 25 seconds be taken off the game clock so that it be in sync with his clock. In a game where every second counted, the decision infuriated Bowman.

"I never understood what the call was, but they did it," says Bowman. "I guess you can't cry over spilled milk."

Even with four minutes there was hope. VanderKelen was passing with ease every time he dropped back in the pocket. McKay said his team's strategy was to pressure VanderKelen with the full front seven, which ultimately left the middle of the field vulnerable. The strategy failed; after frustrating VanderKelen for much of the afternoon, USC no longer could get to Wisconsin's signal caller.

As the Badgers kept firing, Bowman did his part to keep the offensive linemen moving in and out of every play. The ability to concentrate, even under immense pressure, came naturally, he says. "I was always almost autistic in my ability to center once I got to the offensive line and focus on my assignment for that particular play. Forget about the people in the stands, forget about the noise ... this was my job."

After receiving the punt following a safety, VanderKelen moved Wisconsin into the end zone in just three plays, this time finding Richter – who caught 11 passes for 163 yards – to make the score 42-37. But the ensuing onside kick failed and the Trojans were able to milk the clock close to zero, eliminating any hope of a last-second miracle.

Says Bowman, "We felt drained but we also felt that we gave it all we had. The tank was empty. If it wasn't good enough, it just wasn't good enough."

Legendary *Los Angeles Times* columnist Jim Murray described it this way: "The game lasted only slightly less long than the War of 1812. It started in broad daylight but it ended up under conditions so dark a man would bump into an elephant ... USC won, but they were like the kid who comes home with a nose bleeding, his ear torn, his clothes ripped and both eyes black and he says, 'But you ought to see the other fellow.'"

In the first-ever bowl game pitting college football's top two ranked teams, USC and Wisconsin set a new Rose Bowl record for combined points (79), the Badgers set a record for first downs (32) and VanderKelen set a single-game passing mark for yardage (401). Virtually every set of numbers had pointed in Wisconsin's favor except for one.

Offered Bruhn to reporters afterward, "What can I say except that Southern California is truly the No. 1 team in the land? But I have just as much regard for our own – the No. 2. I don't believe I've ever seen a team hang as tight as ours did when things looked black."

As if the loss didn't sting enough, reports surfaced that McKay had told an Associated Press reporter, "They're a good team, but they'd finish about sixth in our league." McKay later denied making the statement, but by then his words had travelled back to Madison.

The Badgers were deflated. The long trip to California, the stay at the monastery and the failed comeback attempt had all taken a toll. "It was certainly not a joyous plane ride back," says Bowman.

Still, through the years the 1963 Rose Bowl has remained one of Wisconsin football's proudest moments, perhaps because Bowman and his teammates didn't give up in that final quarter, or because it is often referred to as one of college football's most thrilling bowl games.

>>>

Even without the 1-2 punch of VanderKelen and Richter, the Badgers were considered a favorite to return to Pasadena the following season ... but it was not to be. The squad opened the year ranked No. 7 and moved up as high as No. 2 after winning its first four games, including a 14-9 victory over Notre Dame. From there, though, things went flat. Ohio State won a tight game at Camp Randall and the Badgers were destroyed by Michigan State the following week. Bowman and his teammates dropped four of their final five contests to finish a disappointing 5-4.

"We were a year older, and presumably a year better, and we should have done a whole lot better than we did," says Bowman, a co-captain that year with Andy Wojdula.

Upon leaving Madison, Bowman was picked in the eighth round of the 1964 NFL Draft by Vince Lombardi's Green Bay Packers.

"I got up there and the biggest adjustment was that Lombardi numbered the holes odd to the right, even to the left. It was the opposite of what we had done in Madison. People say, 'That's not much of a switch' but it was because Bart (Starr) called a lot of audibles."

Of course, Bowman is known best for his double team block with Jerry Kramer against Dallas defensive lineman Jethro Pugh in the Ice Bowl. Their combined effort helped Starr find the end zone to defeat the Cowboys in perhaps the most famous game in pro football history.

But even with the fame that came from being part of Green Bay's glory, Bowman soon discovered that he would need to rely on a career after football.

"After starting for coach Lombardi my rookie year, in 1964, and being an ex-Badger, I thought I was a choice employee candidate and so I waited for the phone to ring. It didn't ring. My choices were to either pound weights in the basement all offseason or get out and do something."

Bowman decided to enroll in law school at Madison, taking whatever courses were available each spring and making up the fall classes later. Often it meant taking courses out of order. "I knew how to sue for breach of contract before I knew what a contract was," he laughs. After seven years, and a few classes at DePaul and Northwestern, Bowman had his law degree. "Not bad for a guy who was a real jerk and didn't study much in high school."

In 1972, the Wisconsin sportswriters voted Bowman the Packers' most valuable offensive player.

"Ed Garvey found that out and said to all of the other player reps, 'You know, to tell how (expletive) the Packers are, they voted a center – Bowman – as their best offensive player.'" The NFL union boss was only ribbing a good friend; the two helped to strengthen the player's union in the early 1970s before most of the post-merger player representatives were forced out of football by agitated owners.

It happened to Bowman in 1974. "They diagnosed a mystic back injury that strangely enough has never resurfaced," he laughs, "and I was waived through the league. I went to Honolulu and played in the World Football League for the Honolulu Hawaiians, just to show there was nothing wrong with my back."

After that, Bowman had an offer to stay in Hawaii and work for the attorney general but instead opted to return to DePere, where he had been neglecting his law office. "If you know anything about offensive linemen, once they start something, they don't quit until it's done."

Bowman stayed put in DePere until he and his second wife relocated to Arizona in 1994. There he found work as a public defender before being appointed to a judgeship. As late as 2010 Bowman was serving the Tucson area as a special magistrate. "It's somewhat of a part-time deal," he says. "If one of the full-time judges is sick, or on vacation, I get called to go in."

And when he doesn't get called in, Bowman is out on the golf course with his wife.

GREGG BOHLIG
1972-1974

The quarterback couldn't believe what his coach was saying. After three seasons of battling through injuries and working his way up the depth chart, now that it was finally his time to take command of the offense, the coach was prepared to go in another direction.

John Jardine just didn't think young Gregg Bohlig was up to the challenge.

Had Jardine forgotten that Bohlig was once the state's player of the year and a Gatorade All-American at Eau Claire Memorial? Jardine had a number of younger quarterbacks on the roster that he was anxious to try out, and after seeing his club finish 4-7 the year prior, was probably desperate to get things turned around. But Bohlig wasn't willing to walk away quietly.

"I've got some stubbornness and competitiveness," says Bohlig, "so I told him I would prove him wrong, went to work and did everything I could do to get better and prove I deserved to be the starter."

All Bohlig had ever wanted was to be the starting quarterback in Madison. After having moved from Minneapolis to Eau Claire's east side prior to fifth grade, Bohlig had been successful in everything he played. He was named to the all-state team in three sports in high school and could have gone pro in baseball had he not been determined to play college football.

The University of Minnesota wanted him badly, even arranged for him to visit campus in September of 1968 to catch a glimpse of O.J. Simpson and the visiting USC Trojans. But Bohlig didn't make that trip – he suffered a concussion the Friday before in a game against La Crosse Central. "I don't remember a thing other than that they wore black uniforms," he says. The concussion put him in the hospital and threatened the rest of his junior season.

Then fate walked through the door. It was Wisconsin Athletic Director Elroy Hirsch, carrying with him a special helmet to limit further concussions. "I think my dentist, Dr. Buzz Mahler, contacted the Badgers athletic department," says Bohlig. Mahler was a University of Wisconsin alum and letter winner who had taken Bohlig to Badger games and was intent on seeing the prep star attend his alma mater. "It was a heavy-duty helmet. It weighed about three times as much as a regular helmet, but I was glad to have it and get back out there and start playing again. I don't know if that was any kind of violation of NCAA rules or not, but it was a unique experience. It made me feel like they had a special interest in me."

After that visit, Minnesota didn't stand a chance.

But Bohlig's first taste of rejection at Wisconsin occurred only a few moments after he stepped foot on campus. "My parents dropped me off at the union where we were supposed to have a team dinner," recalls the 5-foot-11, 175-pound Bohlig. "I was the last guy hanging around in the lobby and I went to go into the meeting and the guy at the door stopped me. He said the meeting was for football players. Obviously, I did not look the part."

Bohlig suffered a bad knee injury early in his freshman season that lingered into the following year. "I'd reinjure it, go in and have it drained and then sit for another couple of months," says Bohlig of the frustration. "My expectations were high and I think the people of Eau Claire expected me to do something and all of a sudden I was the forgotten guy because I was always hurt. It was hard."

Finally healthy for the 1972 season, he jumped from being UW's varsity reserve quarterback to its lead backup in little time. Bohlig saw action in mop-up duty that year – some of it good, some of it not-so-good. He helped however – and wherever – he could.

"Before the Purdue game our kicker had gotten hurt. So, believe it or not, we didn't have a kicker. I had done some kicking in high school – wasn't particularly good at it, but I had kicked – and coach Jardine decided to hold an open contest for the Purdue game. Well, they were using these big ol' balloon balls and I was kicking fairly accurate and ended up winning. So we get to Purdue and we're warming up and Jardine tells me to practice extra points. They've got all these new footballs and they're hard as rocks. So I'm kicking, and I'm nervous, and I'm barely getting them over the crossbar."

Laughs Bohlig, "Obviously it was embarrassing, because Jardine came over and said, 'Forget it, Bohlig, we're going for two.'"

When the year was over, Bohlig was the most experienced quarterback on the roster; he just didn't have Jardine's confidence. Even after spring practice where he had proven he was the most capable man for the job, Bohlig had to keep fighting. "They kept bringing in guys and I kept beating people out. We came into fall camp and I had to win my position again." But he did, and the job was finally his.

Unfortunately, that may have been the high point of Bohlig's junior season. Despite ranking second in the Big Ten in passing and total offense, Bohlig could not get the Badgers over the hump. The team lost a one-point game to Purdue, then dropped tight games to No. 19 Colorado (28-25) and No. 2 Nebraska (20-16). The Nebraska loss was especially frustrating, as Jardine's club had owned a lead at Lincoln for a brief time, only to let it slip away. Wisconsin lost another close game to No. 4 Ohio State (28-20) and was forced to accept another 4-7 season.

Heading into his senior year, UW's quarterback and captain felt he still had plenty to prove – to Wisconsin doubters, to Jardine, and to himself.

GAME I WON'T FORGET

September 21, 1974
vs Nebraska

For four straight seasons Jardine had won four games. The talent was in place – guys like running back Billy Marek, wide receiver Jeff Mack and one of the country's finest offensive lines – but the team wasn't where it wanted to be yet. "Football publications called us a dangerous offensive team with the toughest schedule in the country that year," says Bohlig. "But we felt like we were good enough and could get it done. We were picked for middle of the pack. But we saw it differently."

Things picked up in the first game of the 1974 season against Jardine's alma mater, Purdue. Without Marek, who missed chunks of the season with various injuries, the Badgers played well and won, 28-14. "We hadn't had much success on the road in previous years, so to get that one under our belts was huge," says Bohlig.

The following week the team welcomed Nebraska to Madison. The Cornhuskers had bigger and better-known players, and they were the fourth-ranked team in the country under the guidance of second-year coach Tom Osborne. On offense, Nebraska was led by two of the country's finest: quarterback David Humm, who completed 25 of 36 passes for 297 yards in the 1973 contest, and 1,000-yard rusher Tony Davis, who had caught the winning score in that game.

Jardine downplayed the idea that Nebraska might take his Badgers lightly for a second straight year. "Nebraska is going to practice for us this year," he told reporters, "and not just warm up on Saturday."

Still, every man on the Badgers roster was going to be ready, whether Nebraska was or not.

"You can sense when you're preparing when there is an air of confidence. Our coaches sensed that and had us believing there was no reason we couldn't beat these guys," says Bohlig, "... but we already knew that."

Nebraska grabbed the lead in the first quarter on a Don Westbrook 22-yard touchdown run. But near the end of the quarter the Cornhuskers lost Humm to an injured shoulder. "That was a big factor in the game," says Bohlig. "They had a backup come in who hadn't played much, which I'm sure limited them quite a bit. I'm also guessing they just really didn't expect us to play the way we did."

Wisconsin tied up the game thanks to tight end Ron Egloff's leaping nine-yard touchdown catch in the second quarter, but the half ended on a sour note; a Marek fumble with only a few minutes remaining gave Nebraska an opportunity to regain the lead, this time on a six-yard John O'Leary touchdown.

The second half began much the same way the first ended, with Wisconsin failing to gain much ground. Nebraska added a field goal to claim a 10-point lead, but if the fans in Camp Randall had been deflated, the Wisconsin players had not. The Badgers finally found their footing, and Marek's one-yard plunge at the start of the fourth quarter brought Wisconsin to within three points, 17-14.

Midway through the quarter Nebraska took control of the ball at midfield and drove to the Wisconsin two-yard line, where it was set up to put the contest away. But on first down Rick Jakious, Mike Versperman and Ken Simmons corralled Nebraska fullback Jeff Moran for a three-yard loss. On third down, defensive back Steve Wagner popped Moran again, forcing Nebraska to take the field goal instead of putting the game out of reach.

"It was huge," says Bohlig. "Obviously they had a powerful running game, but our guys were bound and determined to keep them out of the end zone."

On the first play of the next series Bohlig was sacked in his backfield by Nebraska's swarming defense. Faced with a second and 16 from Wisconsin's own 23-yard line, Bohlig dropped back again, this time completing the greatest pass of his career.

Describes Bohlig, "It was a play that wasn't designed to be a touchdown pass. I got out of the pocket and rolled to my right, and Jeff Mack ran a slant pattern. He was supposed to read the safety, and if the safety hung back he was supposed to turn it into an out route and we would complete a 12- to 15-yard play. Instead, the safety jumped the route, so Jeff read it and made a move to get past him. Thankfully, Ken Starch and Billy Marek had knocked down the end, giving me time for it to develop."

Referees threw a flag on the play when the defender bumped Mack, but it didn't matter; the receiver hauled in Bohlig's pass and streaked 77 yards for the go-ahead score.

Commented Mack afterward: "Sure, he bumped me. But he also let me get behind him, and Gregg got the ball out there just where I wanted it. It was a beautiful pass, a beautiful play." It was six points, and Vince Lamia's extra point made it a 21-20 game in favor of Wisconsin.

"It was like manna from heaven," says Bohlig. "Crazy."

Nebraska had one last possession to save face, but Wagner picked off an Earl Everett pass and the Badger offense was able to run off the remaining time on the clock. Chaos erupted on the field and in the streets of Madison. The party afterward was as much news the next day as the Badgers' unthinkable victory.

"It had been hard on all of us to go through some of the tough times we had gone through ... those losing seasons when we were close but weren't getting it done," says Bohlig. "Beating Nebraska felt really good. As a team, we felt it was where we deserved to be." Bohlig was named the *Sports Illustrated* "National Back of the Week" for his performance.

>>>

Wisconsin let a close game slip away the following week against Colorado, then squashed Missouri, 59-20, to set up a showdown in Columbus with top-ranked Ohio State for Big Ten supremacy. Things didn't go as scripted. Says Bohlig, "I lost my poise and had a bad game, probably the worst game I ever played. But I can also say Ohio State was phenomenally good. They just had so many weapons."

Wisconsin also lost close games to third-ranked Michigan and Michigan State but claimed its final three games behind Billy Marek's incredible running to give Jardine the winning season he'd been working for during his time at Madison. Wisconsin's 5-3 conference mark was good for fourth place behind the three teams they had lost to. Bohlig was honored by his teammates as the team MVP, but always felt he "should have handed off that trophy to Billy on the way out of the banquet."

Bohlig was able to leave the school with few regrets, knowing he had worked hard to make the most of a tough situation and helped turn the Badger program in the right direction.

After college the communicative disorders major took a position in Minneapolis area before returning to Eau Claire to take a program position at the YMCA. In the early 1990s Bohlig transitioned to a new job as an agent with State Farm Insurance, the same company his father had worked for during Bohlig's youth. Bohlig and his wife Barbara, whom he met in his freshman year at Madison, raised three athletic daughters, two of whom became UW graduates.

Bohlig's post-Madison athletic achievements almost rival what he accomplished on the football field. He has competed in national tennis and touch-football tournaments and numerous marathons, including the Boston Marathon in 1982 (2 hours, 49 minutes). "I also play a lot of bad golf," he laughs.

Bohlig admits that to this day, almost weekly someone will recognize his name and ask about that win over Nebraska. "It was clearly a significant milestone for Wisconsin football that touched the hearts of many long-suffering Badger fans. I was blessed to be a part of it." Recently, he took a call from a man who wanted the Badgers quarterback to reminisce. "The guy was a diehard Badger fan and remembered as much about that game as I did."

BILLY MAREK
1973-1975

In the early 1970s, Illinois had no state high school football playoffs, just the Prep Bowl, pitting Chicago's finest public school against the winner of the Catholic League. Dating back to 1927 it had long been viewed as the game of the year, attracting close to 50,000 spectators each fall.

For a couple of years the game belonged to coach Pat Cronin's St. Rita squad and its outstanding rushing attack, led by linemen Dennis Lick and Joe Norwick, and the Mustangs' small but powerful back, Billy Marek. With Mayor Richard J. Daley and his entourage in attendance, St. Rita rattled off back-to-back Prep Bowl wins in 1970 and 1971.

Marek and his teammates were stars before they were men.

Growing up in Chicago during the Ara Parseghian era, Marek recalls everything being painted Notre Dame gold. Football was life. "They had a parade almost every weekend before the (grammar school) game. It was the dominant sport and almost everyone in the neighborhood was involved. You wanted to be a part of that."

Marek was unable to play junior high football due to Osgood-Schlatter disease but by ninth grade he was ready to join the team at St. Rita, where he and his freshman teammates allowed few points. Two years later they turned the program around, and Marek walked away as the Catholic League's all-time leading rusher.

Says Marek, "It was a great couple of years, winning against some pretty good public league schools. Just great games."

With that success came a lot of attention from college recruiters. Marek's father worked for a man who happened to be president of the Notre Dame alumni association. And his mother's boss was very well connected with the University of Iowa. There was little chance the St. Rita star was going to escape the Midwest; it was just a matter of where the 5-foot-8 tailback fit best. Eventually, his recruiting compass pointed him a little further north.

"They had Rufus Ferguson but there wasn't a dominant guy behind Rufus and it appeared that Wisconsin might be a better opportunity than the other schools we looked at," says Marek. "Plus, Wisconsin had a coaching staff that was heavily dominated by Chicago people." The Badgers' coach at the time, John Jardine, was a product of the Chicago Catholic League, and a couple of former St. Rita players, Bob Mietz and Danny Schroeder, were already up in Madison. "Wisconsin ran the same offense as my high school, was even the same color," says Marek. "Everything seemed to fit, and the campus was spectacular. There was no downside."

Marek, Lick and Norwick were also taken by Wisconsin's chief recruiter, assistant coach Chuck McBride.

"He was a Chicago guy. Tough, funny, knew everybody," recalls Marek. "Some of the people talking to you would tell you what you wanted to hear. He wasn't like that at all. He'd say something like, 'Don't worry about showing up in shape because there's no way you're going to play as a freshman.' You could see the honesty in his face. And he always had a joke or a story to tell. The kind of guy you wanted to be around."

Like many Chicago Catholic families, Marek's father dreamt of gold-colored helmets, but Marek convinced his father that Madison was a better bet than South Bend.

"I was fortunate he let me make that decision, even though in his heart he would have liked for me to go to Notre Dame. And as it turned out, he was very happy with what happened after. I just didn't feel it was a good fit for me at the time, and I think Wisconsin wanted us in a big way."

As a freshman, Marek carried the ball just one time – a fumble in a 27-7 loss to Illinois.

"The program at that time was still struggling, although they had fabulous players like Mike Webster. Rufus was tremendous. Loved watching him run."

Lick started right away on the line; soon it became Marek's turn.

During spring practice following that season, the eager young back began to work his way through a depth chart that included Duane Johnson and Tony Davis.

"At the end of our freshman year I think Tony hurt his knee, Duane hurt his ankle, another guy hurt his neck and one guy had grade trouble and all of a sudden I was the only tailback still standing in the final two weeks of spring practice. And Kenny (Starch) was the only fullback still standing, so we wound up finishing camp as 1-2. And when we came back in the fall, things started where they had ended and it just stuck. It was as much about luck as it was opportunity."

Another fortuitous thing happened prior to Marek's sophomore campaign – the Badgers hired Ellis Rainsberger to be the new offensive coordinator. "He was tremendous," says Marek. "You'd run a play in practice and he'd tell you that you're foot started off in the wrong direction, your shoulders were turned wrong – so specific."

In 1973, Marek posted the first of three consecutive 1,200-yard seasons, including a pair of 200-yard efforts (Wyoming and Iowa). "It was probably the most enjoyable year. You're a sophomore and you don't know anything and you don't worry about anything. You just use your instincts and run."

The Badgers barely lost to Colorado, Nebraska and Minnesota that year, a sign that change was on the horizon for Jardine's emerging squad.

GAME I WON'T FORGET
November 23, 1974
vs Minnesota

Marek's junior season presented one test after another for Wisconsin. After discarding Purdue, the Badgers upset No. 4 Nebraska. "Just a tough, physical game," says Marek. "Defensively, I think it was one of our best efforts. You watch that film and the defense was just awesome."

Wisconsin let a win slip through its fingers at Colorado before returning home to beat Missouri soundly, 59-20. Then came the top-ranked Buckeyes. "Ohio State was loaded, top to bottom, offense and defense. George Hill was the defensive coordinator and every time we audibled their defense would change. They were in your head and all over you on the field. So big and so fast. I think (Randy) Gradishar grabbed me when I came over the top of one pile and was holding me upside down by my ankles ... 'Umm, can you put me down, sir?'"

The following week Jardine's club lost another game, this time to the No. 3-ranked Wolverines. Says Marek, "Michigan, I always felt we should have beat. That year we were plowing on the field against them." An injury forced Marek to miss the win over Indiana. By this point Starch was leading Wisconsin in rushing, and injuries and fumble trouble had consumed much of Marek's season. Forced to cut a hole in his Riddell cleats to ease the pain of turf toe, Marek was anxious to get back on the field to help the Badgers finish the conference season.

Marek gained 206 yards against Iowa, then broke his own school record with a 230-yard day against Northwestern. "Those last three or four games, we were marching up and down the field," says Marek. "It was incredible how we were moving the ball."

All that remained was the season finale against Minnesota.

In those years, recalls Marek, Minnesota was always a tough, physical affair. In fact, he got knocked out of the junior varsity game against the Gophers his freshman season – the only time in his prep or collegiate career that he left a game without all of his senses. He and his line mates were confident they could do to the Gophers what they had done to the Hawkeyes and Wildcats. It was just a matter of whether the offense could do enough. "It was one thing to score points, which we could always do," he says, "but it was another thing to stop people."

The field conditions that November afternoon were hardly ideal; it was a damp and misty day and the playing surface was slick. The Gophers had trouble staying upright, which gave the sure-footed Marek an advantage.

After Minnesota's Rick Upchurch took the opening kick back 100 yards, the Badgers settled in for a 72-yard drive capped by a short Marek touchdown plunge. After another Minnesota score, Wisconsin quarterback Gregg Bohlig hit Randy Rose on a 48-yard pass to knot the score again. Then Marek took command, rattling off one long run after another. His 35-yard touchdown gave Wisconsin its first lead; a two-yard score shortly thereafter gave the Badgers a 28-14 edge at halftime.

"Our offensive line was just taking them apart," says Marek. "I had huge, gaping holes. And when I did make contact, they weren't tackling well because they were slipping and sliding. I remember one guy sliding past me, yelling 'Get that little son of a bitch.'"

In the second half, Marek padded Wisconsin's lead with a 32-yard run that all but took Minnesota out of contention. Seemingly corralled by Minnesota's Ollie Bakken and Doug Beaudoin, Marek somehow broke free, later telling reporters of the play, "I was turning and I didn't feel anybody still holding me. I don't know what happened, you'll have to ask them (the Gophers)."

The Wisconsin faithful gave the tailback multiple standing ovations and chanted 'We want Marek' over and over again.

And more is what they got … a team-record 43 carries.

One scoring run was brought back due to a penalty, negating more than 65 yards from Marek's total. "Another run I'll never forget: We were on our five-yard line and I broke one down the middle of the field and it was the only time in my career when I felt like I was running out of gas. The guy had a pretty good angle and got in front of me, and I was pretty tired and didn't do everything I could have done to get rid of that guy. It was one of the most frustrating plays in my life. I had felt like I had let myself down. To this day I think of it clearly, quite often."

With the clock winding down and the game well in hand, Jardine kept feeding his workhorse. Says Marek, "I couldn't understand because the score was so lopsided and we had put up a lot of yards. That's when somebody said I was close to 300 yards. Up until then I was just playing, not paying attention. When you're slipping and sliding, banging heads, it's a lot of fun. A lot of fun!"

In all, Marek gained 304 yards – a Badger record that stood for more than two decades – and scored five times in the 49-14 romp, tying a Big Ten record originally set by the great Red Grange in 1924. Marek also tied former Penn State running back John Capelletti's national record by posting three consecutive 200-yard games.

Wisconsin's defense was also special in the contest. The unit pressured Gophers quarterback Tony Dungy and collected its share of Minnesota's five turnovers. The win also helped the Badgers finish 1974 with a 7-4 mark – the first time in more than a decade the program had achieved a record above .500.

Marek was gracious on his greatest collegiate day. He offered kudos to his splendid line and to his fullback, Starch. "Sure, I got the yards," Marek told reporters from his locker, "but this was a great team job."

>>>

The pieces were in place for Wisconsin to have another exciting run in Marek's senior season of 1975, but the Badgers suffered from two key departures: Bohlig and Rainsberger.

"We wanted to pick up where we left off, but we never really did find a replacement for Gregg Bohlig. I think we had a different quarterback practically every game for a while," says Marek. "And there was a co-offensive coordinator situation that was different. It just never seemed to work out. It was one frustration after the next."

That season, Jardine matched the four-win total he had posted in his first four seasons at Madison and everything seemed to fall back to where it had been before.

"We knew we were a better team than we were showing," says Marek, who points out that many of his teammates were later picked up by NFL franchises: Ron Egloff by the Broncos, Dennis Lick by the Bears, Terry Stieve by the Saints, John Reimer by the Oilers, and Ken Starch by the Packers. "Look at all of the power we had on offense. How did we not win more games?"

The season was equally frustrating for Marek, who struggled to regain the footing he had at the end of his junior season ... quite possibly because he didn't have the right attire. "After the (1974) season I threw my shoes away, and it was a Riddell shoe they didn't make anymore. I know in the Michigan game my senior year I tripped two or three times when I thought I was about to click off a bunch of yards. And now I look back and wonder, 'I bet it was the damn shoes.' But who knows?"

Marek gained 198 yards against both Iowa and Northwestern later that season, and finished his career with 3,709 yards to surpass Alan Ameche's school record. In the end, the compact tailback owned virtually every Badger rushing record.

After failing to stick in Bears' training camp, Marek began a successful career for a sports outfitting company. Eventually he established his own company, The Competitive Edge, which now handles sales for Reebok and Adidas in 10 states throughout the Midwest. He catches Badger football games as often as he can, and a few years ago hired former team captain Andy Crooks to assist with sales in Wisconsin.

"It's like they always say: If you have a job you really like it's not like working. I've been in the sports business for 30 years and I feel like I've never had a job."

DAVID GREENWOOD
1979-1982

David Greenwood was ready for his recruiting nightmare to end. The Park Falls High School standout's scheduled visits with Colorado and Cal were cancelled for one reason or another, and he had been snowed out of every flight he had planned to take to Ann Arbor to visit the Wolverines. Greenwood's first choice, the University of Minnesota, was suddenly no longer an option after the school dismissed head coach Cal Stoll; the new coach hadn't a clue who Greenwood was, and the prep star just didn't get a good feeling from him during a return trip to the Twin Cities.

Although the University of Wisconsin had been pursuing Greenwood aggressively from the start, he had suffered through several long years of losing football at Park Falls and had little interest in going to a program that had boasted just one winning season between the years 1964 and 1977. Still feeling burdened by the recruiting experience, and frustrated by his failed attempts to get to other campuses, Greenwood finally caved.

"I had told Wisconsin no a few times," says Greenwood. "One assistant coach was heavy on my heels and every time I turned around he was there. Finally, I said yes."

The news did not sit well in Ann Arbor.

"It was weird because as soon as I hung up with Wisconsin I got a phone call from Michigan and proceeded to get chewed up and down by coach (Bo) Schembechler. He screamed in my ear for a good ten minutes when I told him I was going to sign with Wisconsin. He was frustrated, telling me how I better get my butt to Michigan, and if I didn't I'd be sorry because they were going to beat our butts for four years. Being that I'm a loyal guy, I had committed to Wisconsin and told him 'sorry.' After he was convinced I wasn't going to change my mind he slammed the phone down."

Michigan's legendary coach didn't win 234 college games without having an eye for talent. Schembechler, like a lot of other coaches around the country, knew just how good an athlete Greenwood was, and how it would translate to the football field.

In first grade, after accepting some advice from an older sister on where to place his plant foot, Greenwood high jumped four feet. By junior high he had beaten his older brother Tom's high school mark of 5-foot-9, and by the time he graduated high school he was jumping well over seven feet.

In football, Greenwood started at quarterback and free safety his sophomore year, then shifted to running back and middle linebacker. He served as his team's kicker, punter, and kick and punt returner. "I never left the field," he says. Greenwood was an unstoppable force, but he and his Class B Park Falls teammates were regularly pitted against Class A opponents, making his high school football experience "bittersweet."

At Madison, the debate wasn't whether the talented and athletic freshman should play in his first season, but where; Greenwood, who had never played wide receiver before, caught the winning touchdown at an all-star game, and both the Badgers defensive backs coach, Doug Graber, and the receivers coach felt they needed him on their side of the ball.

"Doug Graber won that battle," he says.

Things came quick that first year. In a game against UCLA, Greenwood put such a lick on All-American running back Freeman McNeil that afterward the talented rusher told the freshman so. Says Greenwood, "As a freshman, that's how you get respect."

But respect was hard for him to find in his own locker room. The Badgers were going through a period of transition, and he and fellow freshman Tim Krumrie had earned starting jobs on defense over much more experienced players. It didn't sit well with most of the team's upperclassmen.

"I felt the vibes," says Greenwood, "and they weren't good vibes.

Those guys had built relationships and I wasn't part of the family – until about halfway through the season when I showed what I could do."

The 6-foot-3, 190-pound athlete could do plenty; he not only started in the secondary, but he was the team's best option at punter (where he stayed for his first three seasons at UW).

Throughout 1980, the Badgers defense was starting to earn respect for being one of the best in the Big Ten. The unit was largely responsible for the team's four wins that year, and also for trimming the margins of defeat against conference powerhouses Michigan and Ohio State.

But Greenwood and his teammates were tired of moral victories. The 1981 season, they all figured, had better deliver results with more substance.

GAME I WON'T FORGET

September 12, 1981
vs Michigan

At the start of the 1981 college football season, Bo Schembechler and his club were ranked No. 1 in the country after having won the Rose Bowl the year before. The Wolverines were a well stocked squad, especially on offense, where they boasted explosive passer Steve Smith, returning 1,000-yard rusher Butch Woolfolk, and three linemen who would later be named to the 1981 All-American squad. Michigan's first test that season was Wisconsin; the two schools had commenced both the 1975 and 1976 seasons against one another, with Michigan getting the best of both of those contests.

Greenwood wasn't concerned with any of that. Two weeks prior to the game he had suffered a punctured lung. Even though the media had listed him as questionable, Greenwood was not going to miss the game for the world; his assignment was far too important. "I knew I needed to shut down Anthony Carter and blow him up a few times." Carter was the Wolverines' dynamic wide receiver who would later join Greenwood on the USFL's Michigan Panthers and achieve fame on the Minnesota Vikings. The junior had logged five 100-yard efforts in his first two seasons, and Greenwood was determined to make sure Carter did not add a sixth on this particular afternoon.

Dave McClain and his team were confident they could get the job done despite Michigan's ranking. If anything, it gave the talented Badger defense the advantage of playing the underdog role at home. The unit, stacked upfront with Krumrie and Darryl Sims, had solid players at linebacker and a young cast of cornerbacks to complement safeties Matt VandenBoom and Greenwood in the secondary.

Says Greenwood, "Defensively, we had a lot of swagger because we knew we had some talent. It was just a matter of us being able to put some points on the board. The discussions in and out of practice were pretty cocky."

McClain fanned the flames. "Just like any good coach would do, he tried to get the confidence level peaking before the game," says Greenwood. "You don't want your athletes going on the field thinking they're going to get beat."

The Wolverines scored the game's first points in the second quarter after their coverage unit collected a fumbled punt inside Wisconsin territory. Six plays later, Smith took it in from four yards out. The Wolverines returned one of Greenwood's punts 48 yards on their next possession but missed a field goal try from 46 yards. Capitalizing on the missed opportunity, Badgers quarterback Jess Cole guided his club 71 yards, finishing the drive with a 17-yard pass to Marvin Neal in the end zone – Wisconsin's first points against a Michigan team after suffering four straight shutouts.

Running backs Chucky Davis, who had been academically ineligible the previous season, and Dave Mohapp proved to be a handful for the Wolverines defense, as the two combined for 156 yards on 34 carries. Davis' one-yard score in the closing seconds of the half gave Wisconsin a 14-7 lead.

Midway through the third quarter, Woolfolk finally broke free from the Badger defense, taking a carry 89 yards to tie the score, 14-14. "That run hurt us," says Greenwood, "but we were young enough to bounce back and continue to stick it to them. And as the game went on, we got more confident."

As devastating as it may have been, it was the only big run for Woolfolk all day, and on Michigan's other 34 carries the team gained just 101 yards (2.9 yards per carry). The Badger front seven did a masterful job of controlling the line of scrimmage.

"I don't know if Bo respected us as much as he should have," says Greenwood. "They tried to run us over and once they found out they couldn't do it they tried to put it up in the air a bit."

That didn't work, either. Thanks to a fierce pass rush, Greenwood and the other defensive backs held Smith to three-of-18 passing for 39 yards and three interceptions. Says Greenwood, "Those interceptions were all caused by the pressure we were getting up front and the frustration I know they were feeling ... just like any offense would that was getting shut down."

Adding to Michigan's frustration was the fact that Wisconsin answered every one of the Wolverines' big plays with a big play of its own. Not long after Woolfolk's score, Cole threw a screen pass to John Williams, who took it 71 yards to give the Badgers the lead again.

As for Greenwood's much-hyped battle with Carter, the junior in red and white got the better of his Michigan rival (Carter caught just one pass for 11 yards). At one point, things got ugly between the two; in the second half, Carter came at Greenwood low on a block, infuriating the Badgers strong safety. "I let him know he was going to pay for it – and he did. I jacked him up good, had him on the ground," says Greenwood. "I don't think he played anymore in the game after that. Maybe I scared him. I don't know."

"I wasn't a very nice guy on the football field."

VandenBoom secured his third interception of the day in the final seconds of the contest, preserving the 21-14 victory for Wisconsin; a mob of fans rushed the field.

Thrilled with the win, Greenwood savored it with his teammates for a moment, then sought out a familiar face. "I looked for (Schembechler) after the game and had a chance to smile at him and wave ... Just wanted to let him know that I appreciated the win that day," he laughs.

Schembechler summed up the loss to reporters afterward: "Our problems were simple. Our offense wasn't any good. Our defense wasn't any good. Our kicking game wasn't any good, and our coaching game was poor. When you have those four things going against you, and you only get beat by seven points, it's a miracle."

"We knew Wisconsin was a good football team," he continued. "Obviously, they were better than what everybody thought they were, and, obviously, we were not as good as everybody thought we were."

Beating the No. 1 team in the country was a big deal, says Greenwood, but no one in Wisconsin's locker room viewed the win as being historic. Certainly, no one knew at the time that it would later be remembered as one of the greatest Badger wins of all-time.

"Did it bolster our confidence? Absolutely. Did we walk with more swagger? Yeah. But we didn't feel that. Our coaching staff didn't allow us to. It was nice to party afterward, and on Sunday we were all fighting off a hangover," he says, "but by Monday we were on to the next game. It wasn't like we had won the Super Bowl and the year was over. Our season was just starting."

>>>

The Badgers suffered a 31-13 loss to top-10 ranked UCLA the following week, but rebounded nicely with Big Ten wins over Purdue and Ohio State. It was Wisconsin's first win over the Buckeyes since 1959. "That game was almost more impressive than beating Michigan," says Greenwood. "We just physically took it to them. I remember (quarterback) Art Schlichter at halftime was almost in tears because he wasn't getting his way and we were shutting him down."

The Badgers finished the year 7-5 and qualified for the school's first bowl game since the 1963 Rose Bowl. "Going to the Big Apple was something that a lot of the guys on the team had never experienced. I remember flying into New Jersey – the Garden State Bowl. It was supposed to be beautiful … well, we landed in a dump," he laughs. "A lot of us lost every penny we had in our pockets playing three-card Monte in the street. A group of New Yorkers took it all. We visited Mama Leone's and I remember after the meal we were all looking for the main course. It was a bunch of exotic seafood, which we had never seen before, but where's the substance? Where's the meat? We went away hungry."

The Badgers also felt unsatisfied after the bowl game.

"The weather was so cold and the wind was blowing so hard," he says. "I was practicing a few punts and I remember dropping the ball and whiffing. I was thinking, 'Oh, my gosh. How are we going to manage this?'"

Tennessee scored 21 first-half points and, despite a Badger rally, held on for a 28-21 win. "Physically, we beat them up but they scored more points than we did," says Greenwood, who earned a spot on the Big Ten's first team following his junior and senior seasons.

The player who McClain once called "the best pure athlete we've ever had" was selected by the Michigan Panthers in the first round of the inaugural United States Football League draft in 1983.

Greenwood was given an $800,000 contract for four seasons and helped Michigan defeat Jim Mora's Philadelphia Stars in the USFL title game that year.

In the April 23, 1984 issue of *Sports Illustrated*, writer Rick Telander profiled the Panthers first team all-USFL safety. Two weeks later, Greenwood fell victim to the 'SI curse,' suffering a knee injury that derailed his second season. When the USFL folded, Greenwood spent time with the NFL's Tampa Bay Buccaneers and Green Bay Packers before a brief stint with the Los Angeles Raiders in 1988.

AL TOON
1982-1984

Al Toon cared little for organized athletics while growing up in Virginia and didn't even try out for the local football team until his sophomore year of high school. When the coaches asked what position he wanted to play, Toon really had no clue; he just knew he was finally ready for football.

Only, football wasn't yet ready for him.

"I fully expected to make the team but I didn't. I got cut," says Toon. "That was my introduction to organized athletics." After his coach delivered the news before practice, the 15-year-old was forced to sit by the school and wait for the team to finish up so he could catch a ride back home. Says Toon, the ordeal was terribly frustrating, but he adds, "I wouldn't change it. It was a learning experience and forced me to take a look at myself and figure out who I was and what I was going to do to rectify the situation."

Toon took to track instead, and soon became one of the state's best in the triple jump and high hurdles. When he returned to football the next fall, the varsity team found a spot for him at tight end and defensive end, and colleges began to show interest.

What Toon really wanted was an opportunity to play both sports. He was beginning to enjoy the game of football, but track was where his long-term priorities were. "My goal had always been to represent the United States in the Olympics," says Toon. "That's what I always wanted to do. Everything else, athletically, was secondary to that."

Wisconsin presented such an opportunity. Not only had Dave McClain's staff recruited Toon's teammate, Art Price, the year before, but Toon's high school football coach was the father of Badgers track coach Ed Nuttycombe. After taking just two of his six scheduled college visits, Toon picked Wisconsin and packed his bags.

While Toon thrived in track, he admits it took a while for him to warm up on the football field and for the Badger coaches to warm up to him. "They weren't sure if I was going to be a track guy or develop as a football player," says Toon. "I sensed that toward the end of my freshman year and decided that I would invest a lot more time in my football skills over the summer."

He and former high school teammate Jeff Price spent the off-season throwing the ball back and forth and talking about the receiver position. "He was probably as big of an influence on my receiving skills and developing a passion for that position as anyone, because he was so passionate about it," says Toon. "That summer I became very comfortable catching the ball and understanding how routes are run. I think the coaches were impressed with the leap I had made from my freshman year to the time camp started."

After rotating with another player for the first few games of his sophomore season, Toon found his way into the starting lineup and quickly began to blossom. All through his freshman season Toon had felt incredibly excited – almost overwhelmed – every time he walked down the Badgers tunnel for home games. Now that he was one of the team's featured playmakers, he no longer heard the stadium noise; his thoughts were consumed only with his assignments on the field.

GAME I WON'T FORGET

November 12, 1983
at Purdue

Not until assistant coach Fred Jackson arrived in Madison did Toon fully develop into one of the Big Ten's best wide receivers. Jackson's guidance got him there and helped to transform the Badger offense into one of the conference's best passing attacks.

The former Jackson State University quarterback had spent only a few seasons at Toledo before joining McClain's staff prior to the 1983 season. Immediately, the coach began to shape Toon's raw talent.

"He taught me about the micros of the position," says Toon, "the little idiosyncrasies about running routes, and understanding defenses. He helped me as an individual, and he helped the offense to develop."

Senior quarterback Randy Wright had thrown for 2,292 yards in 1982 and was widely recognized as one of the conference's most dangerous passers. Toon says other receivers, like fellow starter Michael Jones, helped to take some of the attention away from him on passing downs.

"We had three other receivers that were pretty talented, a nice offensive line, nice tight end, our running backs were great, and we had a commander at quarterback who understood the game and how to distribute the ball based on what the defense was giving him," says Toon.

The offense was ready to explode and Badger fans fully expected the season to end in a bowl game, preferably someplace warm.

Toon got better as the season progressed, and against Iowa in early November he recorded his first 100-yard performance – 136 yards in a 34-14 loss that put a damper on Wisconsin's bowl dreams. At 5-4, the team was now focused on winning its remaining games against Purdue and Michigan State. But due to a knee injury that he suffered against the Hawkeyes, Toon's status was in jeopardy for the game in West Lafayette.

"We came in on Monday and I just couldn't practice," says Toon, who had spent most of the week on crutches. "My knee wasn't cooperating, I couldn't run, and it was pretty doubtful that I'd be able to play. The night before the game I remember sitting in my coach's room going over the gameplan. The other guys left and he and I just decided it'd be a game-time decision."

On Saturday, Toon got dressed just like he would before any other contest, took the field and tested out his knee. "I warmed up and it felt OK, so I told my coach I would give it a try. As things got going I didn't feel much pain at all."

Instead, the pain was reserved for Purdue's secondary.

Wisconsin jumped out to a lead, thanks in large part to Toon's 52-yard reception on the Badgers first drive. Running back Gary

Ellerson took the ball from there and punched it in from the two-yard line. In the second quarter both offenses went on a scoring rampage. Purdue quarterback Scott Campbell tossed back-to-back touchdowns to give his squad the lead before Wright hit Toon on a 73-yard bomb – the longest scoring catch of his UW career.

Things slowed down in the contest for Toon, making it easier for him to see the action on the field and make plays. It helped that his mind had been distracted all week by his injury, and also that he was able to perform on a favorable playing surface. "I always loved playing on natural grass," says Toon. "That was one of the things that allowed me to play that game. Grass is just easier on the body."

Purdue added a rushing score to make it 23-21 in its favor at halftime.

Early in the fourth quarter, clinging to a 28-23 lead, Wisconsin faced a fourth and short from just inside the red zone. Instead of taking the points, McClain decided to go for it and watched as Ellerson was stuffed for a two-yard loss. When Wright was intercepted deep in Badger territory on the next drive the Boilermakers capitalized and climbed back in front.

Toon caught passes of 23 and 18 yards on Wisconsin's next drive, which ended with Wright's third rushing score of the contest.

And the see-saw battle continued ...

Trailing 38-35 with just more than two minutes remaining, Wright took command at his own 37-yard line. Several plays into the drive, Toon made a 27-yard circus catch along the Purdue sideline that brought Wisconsin to the 22-yard line. But after gaining eight yards on first down, the Badgers' momentum came to a halt, and the team was faced with a fourth and one with 37 seconds left.

The game and the team's slim bowl hopes were riding on this one play.

Wright faked to Ellerson, then threw the ball to tight end Bret Pearson, who was wide open in the end zone. "We call that a '14 sucker' pass," Wright told reporters. "We knew we were going to run that because the time before we had fourth and one and didn't make it because they blitzed."

The 42-38 victory was the team's highest scoring game of the season and had given McClain a third straight win over the Boilermakers. Wright completed 16 of 33 passes for 313 yards, the bulk of which went to Toon, who averaged 31.5 yards on his eight receptions.

"He was something else," said Pearson of Toon after the game.

True. Toon was in a class all to himself. His 252-yard day set a new Big Ten record.

"It's hard to wrap your head around it when you're that young," says Toon, who admits he had no idea he was closing in on greatness at any point during the contest. "I definitely have more of an appreciation for it now, especially because it was a game I didn't think I would get in."

>>>

After Wisconsin finished up the 1983 season with a 32-0 win over Michigan State, Toon went back to track and began to focus on the 1984 Olympic Trials. He performed well at the conference and NCAA meets and would have qualified for the Trials in the 110-meter high hurdles and triple jump but blew his hamstring.

He had missed his window for the '84 Games and now had a difficult decision to make.

Says Toon, "At that point it was: OK, I can now spend my time focusing on football because there was going to be another four years before the next Olympics." He opted not to compete in track at Madison after that, in part because his hamstring was still in bad shape and he didn't want to compromise both sports.

The Badgers made a change at quarterback in 1984, handing the reins to Mike Howard, who guided the club to another seven-win record. Thanks to a strong finish, including a win over No. 6-ranked Ohio State, the Badgers qualified for the Hall of Fame Bowl, where they lost to Kentucky, 20-19.

"It was a more difficult season for me as a player," says Toon. "The defense made it more difficult for me to get off the line of scrimmage, and I had to work much harder. I caught more passes but my yardage per catch was way down. But my focus was to be consistent and to try to deliver whatever the team needed to win games."

Toon recorded 100-yard games against Missouri, Illinois and Purdue, and also set a new single-season school record for receptions (54).

Following the 1984 season, Toon was one of 11 Badgers selected in the 1985 NFL Draft; he was picked by the New York Jets with the 10th pick in round one.

"The Badgers played in the Garden State Bowl at the Meadowlands my first year," he says. "So it was serendipitous to end up back in New York and playing there."

In his second season, Toon caught three touchdowns in a Week 8 contest against the Saints, then followed it up with a nine-catch, 195-yard and two-touchdown day against Seattle. He earned a trip to the Pro Bowl each year from 1986 to 1988 and led all NFL receivers in receptions (93) during his fourth season. "My first five years in the league were extremely fun," he says. "I had a great time, had a lot of success."

Trauma resulting from too many concussions ended Toon's career prematurely, and after eight seasons, at the age of 29, Toon called it quits with 517 receptions, 6,605 yards and 31 touchdowns.

Toon's greatest athletic contribution may be his and his wife's four children. Son Nick is a standout wide receiver at the University of Wisconsin, while oldest daughter, Kirby, is on scholarship for volleyball at Madison. Another daughter, Molly, accepted a scholarship to play volleyball at Michigan. The couple's youngest child, Sydney, was an All-American club volleyball player in the 15-year-old age bracket. Toon admits he's very proud of all of their athletic accomplishments, but adds, "Character is the thing we really preach in our household."

When he's not busy watching his kids compete, Toon manages his real estate investments.

PAUL GRUBER
1985-1987

During one of Paul Gruber's toughest moments, Badgers coach Dave McClain was there for the high school senior. It's something that still means a lot to Gruber to this day, and was a big reason why the Sauk Prairie High School tight end chose Madison over the other Big Ten schools that were interested in him.

As a young boy, Gruber often attended Badger games with his family. "I can remember watching Billy Marek and Rufus Ferguson – the stars at that time – and I guess when I was in high school was when coach McClain started to have some success."

Gruber grew as a football player – both on the field and in stature – during his final two seasons at Sauk Prairie. "I think I was about 6-4 when I was a sophomore in high school. A skinny kid, probably 185, then just filled out my junior and senior year. By the time I finished high school I was 245."

He first started gaining the attention of college scouts as a junior, when he and his teammates made a trip to the state playoffs. After that Minnesota and Michigan State came calling; McClain's staff, too. But in his senior year Gruber's father passed away – a tough moment for any son, let alone someone just 17 years old. Instead of treating Gruber like a recruit through the ordeal, McClain understood he was just a kid who needed some support. "I was close to coach McClain through that," says Gruber. "It played a big part in me coming to Madison."

Early into his freshman season, the coaching staff moved the tight end to defensive line, where he struggled and felt out of place. Gruber missed being on the offensive side of the ball. Mostly, he missed working with line coach Ron McBride. "Just a great coach, a great person," says Gruber. "He had a dynamic personality. He expected a lot out of his players but he made it fun."

It was McBride who got Gruber back on offense, convincing the lanky freshman to give the guard spot a try. "I was just trying to find a position where I could play and work my way into a starting role," says Gruber. "Ron gave me the techniques and turned me into a good offensive lineman. There are a few guys who stand out in your mind that got the best out of you, but in a way that makes you want to go to work, and Ron was one of those guys."

In 1985, after two seasons at guard, Gruber made the move to tackle and jumped into the starting lineup. McClain's offense was a good fit for his athleticism. "At that time in football, everyone ran a 3-4 defense. So McClain's system was very much a pro style offense to counter that. It was a good feeding system into the NFL, and if you look at the history, there were a lot of his guys who got drafted and played in the NFL."

Because McClain relied on formation strength to dictate direction, the team did not have a left or right tackle. Gruber served as the team's weakside tackle, rarely if ever lining up next to a tight end. "It was good because I could play out of a right- or left-handed stance."

The 1985 season was expected to be one of transition for McClain and his club. Eleven players had been drafted by NFL teams that spring, including three in the first round. The offensive line had been completely revamped, and the only real carryovers from the offense were running back Joe Armentrout and quarterback Mike Howard.

The team could have packed it in and waited for 1986 to arrive, but McClain wouldn't hear of it. The coach hadn't had a losing season since 1980 and fully expected the 1985 squad to go to a bowl game. "That was the expectation he set year in and year out," says Gruber.

And after three relatively easy non-conference wins, McClain saw no reason to hedge his bet. But the next week the Badgers were pounded by No. 5 Michigan; then they fell short at home, 23-13, to top-ranked Iowa. Those two games began a string of bad breaks, including a three-point loss to Northwestern and a seven-point loss to Illinois. At 4-5, the Badgers were no longer in bowl contention and needed a pair of wins just to finish above .500.

To start, all they needed to do was upset No. 3 Ohio State in Columbus.

GAME I WON'T FORGET
November 16, 1985
at Ohio State

When Ohio Stadium was constructed in the 1920s, its chief designer had dreamt of a horseshoe-shaped arena. For college football fans, it's one of the country's great landmarks; for opposing players, it can be an intimidating place to go to battle.

"For a 20-year-old kid ... I don't want to say overwhelming, but I was definitely in awe," says Gruber. "Their locker room at that time was outdated, with these wooden chairs, concrete floor – what you'd expect from an old school-like environment."

If the atmosphere wasn't enough of an advantage, the Buckeyes had an 8-1 record that season and were riding a 20-game winning streak at the Horseshoe (their last loss to Wisconsin in 1982).

But Ohio State coach Earle Bruce was not about to allow his club to overlook a Wisconsin team that had beaten the Buckeyes in three of the last four meetings. "They're not the Sisters of the Poor," he told a reporter.

One thing that would help Wisconsin was the shape the Buckeyes were in entering the contest. The team was without its Heisman-worthy running back Keith Byars, who was still nursing an injured foot, and linebacker Eric Kumerow, who had a shoulder injury. Several other Buckeye players, including linebacker Pepper Johnson, were suffering from the flu.

All week, McClain had convinced his young squad that not only did it stand a chance of winning the game, but that he believed it would. To do so, though, would require a few breaks.

In the early going, Wisconsin earned its points thanks to a pair of Todd Gregoire field goals. But Ohio State answered just before the half on a long touchdown pass from Jim Kasatos to Cris Carter. Even without Byars, the Ohio State offense was out to prove it was still the best in the Big Ten.

The Buckeyes' defense was considered every bit as good as their offense. Led by Johnson and defensive tackle Chris Spielman, the unit had held both No. 20 Minnesota and No. 1 Iowa to fewer than 20 points. Wisconsin's rag-tag offense was going to be a cinch, or so the majority of the 89,873 fans in attendance figured.

But no matter how good Ohio State's offense or defense was, it didn't matter if Wisconsin was able to win the war it was waging. "In an environment like that, the key to winning is not turning the ball over and running the ball," says Gruber. "And that's what happened – our defense created turnovers and our offense didn't."

To be precise – Wisconsin didn't lose a fumble, while Ohio State lost three. All were recovered by Michael Reid, who had recently shifted from the inside linebacker spot to the outside.

Reid's first fumble recovery came late in the third quarter following a bad quarterback-to-running back exchange. Four plays later Marvin Artley punched it in from a yard out to give the Badgers a 12-7 lead (the two-point attempt failed).

Early into the fourth quarter, Reid pounced on a fumble at the Wisconsin three-yard line when Roman Bates failed to secure the ball, ending what could have been a go-ahead drive for the Buckeyes. On Ohio State's next possession, Reid secured his third fumble after teammates Charlie Fawley and Craig Raddatz popped it free from Ohio State tight end Ed Taggart's hands.

On another second half possession, Wisconsin stopped Vince Workman on fourth down at the Badgers' 11-yard line, again keeping points off the board.

The clock kept ticking, and Wisconsin somehow kept its 12-7 lead. For the fourth time in McClain's tenure, his Badgers had upset the Buckeyes.

The game belonged to the defense, which held Ohio State to just 102 rushing yards, and to the offensive line, which helped Wisconsin to control the ball for more than 34 minutes.

Artley may have scored the Badgers' lone touchdown, but the offense relied on its top back Larry Emery as it had done for much the rest of the season. Emery – who had needed 17 yards at the start of the game to become the first Badger running back in 10 years to eclipse the 1,000-yard mark – carried the ball 28 times for 85 yards and caught three passes for 18 yards. "As an offensive lineman, it's always your goal to have a 1,000-yard rusher behind you," says Gruber, "and to have Larry Emery reach that goal was significant, as well."

After the game, a reporter asked Emery if he had planned to treat his linemen to dinner to celebrate the milestone. "I don't think I have enough money," he said, "as much as those big guys eat."

Gruber took in the post-game celebration and shared a few choice words with the Buckeyes players, including Spielman, who he would later face numerous times while the two men started for opposing teams of the NFC Central Division.

In describing the defeat afterward, all Spielman could say to reporters was, "It was crushing. I won't sleep tonight."

Says Gruber, "I think they were all a little humbled. Maybe they overlooked us a little bit."

McClain thought so. "What helps make this such a sweet victory is that nobody gave us a chance. Not even people in Wisconsin."

It was McClain's last victory as the Badgers coach; the following April he died of cardiac arrest at the age of 48. In eight seasons he had won 46 games, lost 42 and tied three. Only Milt Bruhn and Phil King had won more games for Big Red.

"I remember the day pretty well," says Gruber. "We had just finished spring football. I heard it on the radio driving to the stadium for a workout. He had been a role model for me, especially in light of my father's death. He had gone out of his way to reach out to me during a difficult time."

Commented Wisconsin Athletic Director Elroy Hirsch, "We lost more than an outstanding coach. He was a great father, husband and human being. People like this are not replaced."

>>>

In many ways, that Ohio State game was the last highlight of Gruber's successful career at Madison. After McClain's passing, the school hired defensive coordinator Jim Hilles on an interim basis for the 1986 season. "A lot of the guys that were my friends on that team had graduated," says Gruber, "so it was another transition year where a number of guys were supposed to step up." Regardless of the situation, fans were unhappy the squad won just three games (the program's fewest since 1969) and Hilles was shown the door.

"I don't know if it was the right decision not to give him more time in that position. It's difficult when you're in an interim situation to be successful. But obviously it was just a tough situation."

The following year the program turned to Don Morton, who had built successful programs at North Dakota State and Tulsa. Morton switched to the veer offense, which didn't suit Gruber. The Badgers struggled to make the transition and again won just three games.

"That was a frustrating year," says Gruber. "The players that had been recruited by the previous regime didn't fit in Morton's system."

As bad as things got in Madison, it didn't prevent the Big Ten from naming Gruber to its first team after his senior year, nor did it affect how NFL scouts viewed Gruber, who was selected fourth overall in the 1988 NFL Draft by the Tampa Bay Buccaneers.

"The three teams I had spent the most time with going into the draft were the Lions, Buccaneers and Raiders," says Gruber, "and of them the team I wanted to go to most were the Buccaneers. They had drafted (quarterback) Vinny Testaverde the year before and still had James Wilder, who was a very solid running back. I had spent a lot of time with their coach, Ray Perkins, and felt like they were an up-and-coming team."

Gruber and his teammates struggled through losing seasons in his first nine years in the NFL before Tony Dungy helped to rebuild the franchise. In 1997 the team made the playoffs and in 1999, Gruber's final season, Tampa Bay won the NFC Central for just the third time in franchise history.

In 12 NFL seasons Gruber started 183 games for the Buccaneers at left tackle and was selected to a number of annual teams.

Gruber married his wife, Brenda, before his senior season at Madison. The couple have raised their two sons, Blake and Chase, and daughter, Ashlyn, in the mountains just outside of Vail, Colorado. "It's been a great place to raise a family," he says. Gruber manages his real estate investments and in his spare time hunts elk, rides motorcycles and goes skiing.

Even though his collegiate career ended on a sour note, he is still fond of his time at Madison.

"I loved going to school there," he says. "Big Ten football is very special, and Camp Randall is an awesome environment to play football in. You can't beat it anywhere."

JOE PANOS
1991-1993

It was the afternoon of January 2, 1990, and University of Wisconsin-Whitewater defensive lineman Joe Panos was sitting in front of the television with his roommates watching Barry Alvarez get introduced as the new coach of the Wisconsin Badgers.

"I can remember it like it was yesterday," says Panos. "He had said there'd be open competition for everybody and I told my two roommates that I was going to see if they'd take me as a walk-on." Panos made a call to the team's new defensive coordinator, Dan McCarney, then wrote the school a letter. "In the closing I wrote that I knew I could be a Badger. And coach McCarney said, 'C'mon over kid.'"

The son of Greek immigrants, Panos grew up wanting to be a football player. Through elementary school, middle school and high school, Panos never wavered on his life's dream. "The older I got the more ridiculous it sounded. But I kept on saying it," says Panos. "Everybody else kept changing what they wanted to be but I wasn't willing to give that up."

A solid player for Brookfield East, Panos was somewhat dumbfounded when he got to the end of his prep career and found that virtually no college wanted him. Carthage had shown some interest, but that was it. "I had to call up a buddy who knew the head coach at Whitewater. It was kind of aggravating because I had gone to the UW football camps when Don Morton was the coach and had seen the kids they were recruiting – some of them were from my conference – and I figured I was just as good as these guys. Why wasn't I getting a sniff?"

The opportunity to be a Badger was all Panos had wanted and, walk-on or whatever, he was determined to make it work. But early on he learned that making the transition wouldn't be easy.

"I was doing a drill called county fair on that first day of training camp. It was a bunch of drills you had to do before practice even really got going, just to gas you and get you ready. Anyhow, I was doing something wrong and coach (Bernie) Wyatt said, 'If you keep doing it that way kid you better get your ass back to Whitewater because that doesn't work at this level.' It was a quick lesson of what I needed to do to be successful."

Panos had no trouble with the ribbing he got from Wisconsin's coaches.

"The staff was extremely high energy – aggressive, young, 'Type-A' guys – and they weren't yelling for the sake of yelling. They were coaching. Do-it-my-way-or-get-the-hell-out-of-line kind of guys. I did well under that kind of coaching."

Panos recalls that Alvarez was also realistic about where the team needed to go and how it was going to get there.

"We were in the first meeting and two of the seniors came up and said, 'If you don't think we're going to go 12-0 you can get the hell out of here' and coach Alvarez stopped them. He said you guys haven't won 12 games in six years. Let's have some realistic goals. Coach had a plan, and it was the first thing I caught on to."

At first, Panos stuck on the defensive side of the ball. But injuries were thinning the offensive line, so every practice he'd work both sides to help out. At the end of the year offensive line coach Bill Callahan approached him about the possibility of making the switch to offense permanent. Panos was all ears to the opportunity. He began the following spring as the No. 2 center, then won the starting job, then made a move to guard, and ultimately to tackle.

Heading into the 1993 season, Panos says the team knew it had the potential to do something special. The players all stayed in Madison that summer, and Panos served as their host most of the time.

"I've never been around a team that was so anti-clique," he says. "I had a house that everyone hung out at. We partied together and we hung out there together. It was unbelievable. The O-line hung out with the defensive backs, it didn't matter – race, religion – there were no lines. It was one unit. We did everything together."

It was all part of Alvarez's plan. "Coach had said to me, 'I want you to be the pulse of the team. If anybody is complaining let me know about it so we can fix it.'" Panos was the perfect choice to serve as captain for a team that was on the brink of greatness.

Because the offensive linemen looked as though they were fresh off a construction site, Alvarez often affectionately referred to them as the lunch pail crew. The unit pulverized opponents all year; in fact, in four games that season running backs Brent Moss and Terrell Fletcher each gained more than 100 yards rushing.

In Panos' eyes, by mid-season the team looked the part of a champion.

"We started to experience victories and were feeling good about ourselves, rightfully so. After the Indiana game (reporters) asked me who had a shot at the Rose Bowl and I said 'Why not Wisconsin?' It wasn't empty rhetoric, it was something I truly believed. Where were we weak? Were we weak at running back with Moss and Fletcher? Were we weak at quarterback with Darrell Bevell? Were we weak at the offensive line where four of the five guys ended up playing in the NFL? Were we weak on the defensive side where we had guys like Lamark Shackerford? I believed it, and I think a lot of people on the team believed it."

By the end of October, the club was 6-1 heading into its biggest test thus far: Michigan. The Badgers wore down the Wolverines just like they had done to almost every other team, then for a brief while celebrated a 13-10 victory. In the madness of it all, fans from the student sections of the stadium rushed the field, crushing many of those who were pinned up against the retaining wall.

"There were so many doggone people on the field," says Panos. "I turned to my buddy Brian Patterson and said, 'It's getting chaotic, we've got to get out of here.' And as we were going through the tunnel, that's when we saw the chaos. There were people on the ground bleeding and crying. So me and Brian and a couple of other guys jumped in and tried to do what we could to help these people out. I'm not going to lie, it was the scariest scene I'd seen in my life. You pull somebody out and they're blue in the face, their eyes are rolled over, they've urinated themselves, you didn't know if they were alive. It went from the ultimate high to the ultimate low."

More than 70 fans were treated at local hospitals afterward. It remains one of the darkest days in Badger football history.

After a tie with Ohio State, the Badgers arrived in Champaign for a late game against the Illini. Before the team exited the bus, Alvarez informed them that Michigan had just beaten Ohio State, and that Wisconsin once again controlled its own destiny.

Says Panos, "They could have called the game right then and there, Illinois didn't have a chance. Not a chance. I've never seen 100 guys come off a bus like that in my entire life. I hope I don't sound too smug, but that's how confident we were. A bunch of barking dogs on a chain." The Badgers won 35-10, then two weeks later hopped on plane headed for Tokyo where the team needed one more win against Michigan State to clinch a share of the Big Ten title and a trip to the Rose Bowl.

Says Panos, coach Alvarez was the ultimate preparer. "He had contacted NASA. He had us walking around during the day with shades on, and at night our lights were on. We were practicing at midnight. It was all mental so that there were no excuses. 'You guys are prepared; now you have to go out and execute.' And it worked."

The Badgers destroyed the Spartans, 41-20. Next stop: Pasadena.

GAME I WON'T FORGET

January 1, 1994
vs UCLA

Panos freely admits he wasn't interested in the sights California had to offer, just the game. "The Disneyland thing was annoying," he says. "I had to do some photo opps on a tea cup with Terrell Fletcher. It was just the worst thing. I didn't want to do any of that. But I was being a good soldier."

One thing he and his offensive line mates didn't mind was the Lawry's Beef Bowl. The team that consumed the most steak won the contest; Panos and his teammates not only won, they set a new record.

Disrespect seemed to be the theme that week in Pasadena. Not only were the No. 9-ranked Badgers underdogs to the No. 14-ranked Bruins, but UCLA made no bones about speaking its mind to the media. They weren't the least bit worried about Wisconsin's physicality, their players told reporters, and also that Wisconsin had no idea what it was in store for. "It pissed us off," says Panos.

It got worse.

During the pre-game coin toss, the referee addressed both teams before having Rose Bowl grand marshal William Shatner do the honors. The referee announced UCLA, then *Washington*. "It's Wisconsin," a noticeably annoyed Panos snapped back. Then again, after UCLA had won the toss and deferred, the referee signaled that *Washington* would gain first possession of the ball.

"I said, 'It's Wisconsin, blank, blank, blank.' I dropped a bunch of bombs on him because I was really irritated. Very, very pissed off," says Panos. "I grabbed the offense and said, 'These guys don't even know our frickin' name.' Let's show them who Wisconsin is.'"

The Badgers took the ball on their first drive and pounded Moss behind an offensive line that the Bruin defenders would get to know well that day – tackles Mike Verstegen and Panos, guards Joe Rudolph and Steve Stark, and center Cory Raymer. The drive stalled near midfield, but the message was well understood: We're Wisconsin and we're going to be coming at you all game long.

After UCLA scored a field goal following an 87-yard drive, the Badgers took the ball and again unleashed their power running game on the Bruins defense. Moss for a handful, Moss for a handful more. A dump pass to Moss for five, another Moss carry for 11 ... when Moss finally plunged into the end zone he had touched the ball six times on a nine-play drive that had covered 78 yards. UCLA's fine linebacking corps, which featured future NFL players Donnie Edwards and Jamir Miller, seemed helpless in trying to contain Wisconsin on the ground.

Says Panos, "It's like coach always said, 'Let's take care of our business and let us dictate how the pace of the game goes.' We knew eventually we would wear these guys down."

Bruins quarterback Wayne Cook threw an interception, followed immediately by a Bevell interception, followed by a J.J. Stokes fumble in the open field. After the turnover melee the Badger offense settled in again, grabbed their lunch pails and went back to work.

The team took the ball all the way down to the two-yard line, but Moss got tripped up on first and second down – each time by his own cleats. On third down, Rudolph pulled to the right and Moss followed, squeezing through the hole to put Wisconsin up 14-3.

Moss finished the half having touched the ball 24 times. By

game's end the junior would have 158 yards on 36 carries. In terms of team dominance, Wisconsin's offense collected 15 first downs in the half while UCLA gained only six, and the Badgers had controlled the ball for 18:31 as compared to UCLA's 11:29.

The halftime atmosphere in the Wisconsin locker room was controlled, says Panos. No one was overly excited because each man knew 30 minutes of clock remained. "We knew we had to go out there and put those guys away. And we knew that meant taking care of our business one play at a time, working hard one play at a time, and doing our jobs one play at a time."

The biggest play of the second half wasn't a Moss run, but rather the most unlikely player on the Badgers side of the ball. After the Badgers defense collected a fumble, Bevell rumbled 21 yards to give Wisconsin a 21-10 lead with roughly 11 minutes remaining in the final quarter.

"How long was that run?" Panos jokes. "Seemed more like 80 yards." The senior lineman was the first to greet Bevell in the end zone, lifting up the sophomore high into the air.

Not long into UCLA's ensuing possession – and just moments after ABC commentator Keith Jackson had uttered of the Bruins, "They've run out of feet to shoot" – wide receiver Kevin Jordan fumbled again, handing possession back to Wisconsin. It was UCLA's sixth turnover of the contest.

Despite all of its troubles, UCLA's offense kept ticking. The Bruins scored another touchdown to make it 21-16, and after the Badgers failed to control the ball and run out the clock, the Bruins had one more crack at it with two minutes to go.

"It was like a sundial, that's how slow it was," says Panos of UCLA's final drive. "But we had the utmost confidence in our defense."

Cook and the Bruins offense kept collecting first downs to stop the clock, the last of which went to Stokes, who caught 14 passes in the game to break Pat Richter's Rose Bowl record from 1963. But with the ball at Wisconsin's 18-yard line, Cook panicked and took off running when the pocket collapsed. The Bruins were out of timeouts and unable to get another snap off before the clock ran out.

Alvarez lifted both of his arms in the air triumphantly; the Badger sideline went crazy. When a Rose Bowl official handed Alvarez the trophy afterward, it was Panos who was asked to represent his team next to the coach on the stage.

Sideline reporter Lynn Swann asked Alvarez whether he was

surprised UCLA had coughed up the ball six times (the Bruins entered the game with a positive 19 in turnover margin). "Maybe our defense had something to do with that," the coach replied with a grin. Really, it didn't matter *why* UCLA hadn't been able to hold onto the ball; as Alvarez put it to Swann, "that's football" and on this day Wisconsin was happy to take whatever breaks came its way.

Not until the game was over and he was celebrating with his teammates did it sink in for Panos – his long journey from Whitewater to Madison, from walk-on to captain, from a 1-10 record to the toast of Pasadena. "In the locker room after the game I was a mess," he says. "I think I've cried three times in my life and that was one of them. I couldn't believe we were Rose Bowl champs. It was the coolest thing in my 23 years. One of the best feelings I've ever had."

>>>

The win electrified Badger Nation. Suddenly, everyone in Wisconsin was clad in red, and the Badgers were the topic of choice. "Was I surprised? No, just because Wisconsin was dying for a winner," says Panos. "We knew how crazy the state was getting when we went to Japan and saw the craziness on State Street afterward. And there were 30,000 people waiting for us when we got back. It was awesome."

After the Rose Bowl, "Everything was Badgers this and Badgers that," he says. "For the longest time I didn't pay for my own dinner. And to this day people come up to me and thank me."

Panos had never really thought about playing football professionally until one of Alvarez's assistant coaches, Jim Hueber, told Panos he believed the tackle had a shot. Panos took the compliment to heart and later benefited from the exposure he got from playing in the Hula Bowl, East-West Shrine Game and the Senior Bowl.

A third round pick by Philadelphia in 1994, Panos played six seasons in the NFL – four with the Eagles and two with the Bills.

At the end of his career, Panos coached high school football for a while at Brookfield Central, where he had a chance to work with future Badgers Joe Thomas and Ben Strickland. Later, he started Next Level, a Milwaukee-based training facility that offered athletes a first-rate workout environment. The greatest joy he took from that venture, he says, was seeing kids who had gone through the training end up at Madison and have productive careers.

Today, the father of three continues to support Wisconsin athletics whole heartily.

"I'm a Badger," says Panos, "and I always will be a Badger."

DARRELL BEVELL
1992-1995

Playing for his father at Arizona's Chaparral High School, young Darrell Bevell was enjoying the start of his final season. He had performed well on the field and was collecting letters from a number of interested colleges. But in the third week of the season – in a game against the school from where he had transferred two years before – Bevell shattered a knuckle on his throwing hand on the helmet of another player. His prep career was over.

"All of the letters all of a sudden stopped," he says. Only a few schools were still interested, and of them Northern Arizona was the best choice. There Bevell was first introduced to Brad Childress, the school's quarterbacks coach. "He was very demanding and expected my best all the time, wasn't going to take anything less," says Bevell of his position coach. "I was the son of a coach, so I could be coached hard. I could take anything thrown at me."

The following October, Bevell left for a Latter Day Saints mission and missed a total of three collegiate seasons. To his surprise, his stock had gone up considerably during his absence, all based on Childress' recommendation. Northern Arizona was still recruiting him, as was Utah where the offensive coach had spent a season before accepting an offer to join Barry Alvarez's staff in Madison. "I didn't know how much of an impression I had made on him until I left after that first season," says Bevell.

Bevell liked the fact that Utah was so close to home, but felt compelled to make a visit to Madison in the winter of 1992 to see what Childress, Alvarez and the Badgers program had to offer. "I got off the plane and didn't even have a coat," he laughs. "Got there in January and the snow was rather deep and it was rather cold."

The coaches borrowed Bevell a coat for the weekend and took him and a few other recruits to a hockey game, then offered Bevell their pitch. He bought every word of it. "My only request was to get No. 11 and they said they could work that out so I pretty much committed on the spot right there," he says. "I think I realized that coach Childress had really gone to bat for me and was the reason the other schools were interested in me."

Upon returning home he shared the news with the staff at Utah. "The coach asked, 'Are you sure you want to be that far away from home?' and I said, 'No, I don't want to be that far away but I love the place and it's where I want to go."

Bevell packed his things and returned to Madison, where he quickly learned just how rusty and out of shape he was.

"When you add it all up, I didn't play in a game for five seasons," says Bevell. "I came in and I was way out of shape. I spent those two years (on the mission) driving in a car, riding around on a bike and walking."

"I think at one point coach (John) Dettmann said I had the strength base of a dishrag," he laughs. "I was starting from ground zero."

During the winter workouts prior to the 1992 season Bevell couldn't finish the pre-practice warmup drills. "I just about blew my legs up. That's how bad of shape I was in. They basically put me on what I called the cross country team. While they were doing those stations they had me jogging around the field. It took a couple of months."

Eventually Bevell found his legs, then found his way into the starting lineup.

GAME I WON'T FORGET
January 1, 1994
vs UCLA

For Bevell, the journey to Pasadena really began in Evanston, Illinois at the end of the 1992 season. The Badgers were 5-5 entering that contest, with hopes of earning the first bowl bid of the Alvarez era. Late in the game, and trailing Northwestern by two points, Bevell led the club on a drive that took them into field goal range.

"We wanted one more play just to center the ball," he recalls. "We ended up fumbling the ball and the game was over. I remember the Northwestern guys, particularly their quarterback, popping off to our guys, saying stuff like 'You're not going anywhere, you're staying home with us.' I think it was the first time where our guys could see we had opportunities."

The majority of the team's roster stayed in Madison that next summer and did everything together, says Bevell. It was just the team – total focus, no distractions.

When Alvarez got in front of the group during one offseason meeting he set the coming year's goals. "He just said, 'Our goal is to get to a bowl game and win the game.' He didn't say the Rose Bowl, just a bowl game."

The Badgers won their first four games of 1993, then demolished Northwestern, 53-14, during Homecoming week. A little revenge, perhaps? "That was without a doubt what that game was," says Bevell. "They still had the same quarterback and we remembered it. Our defense took it to them, and the offense played very well."

Purdue was a breeze but the Badgers were dealt their first loss at Minnesota, dropping them to 6-1. Bevell had injured his hip late against Purdue and reinjured it against Minnesota, yet stayed in the game. It was, by his estimation, the worst game of his career (five interceptions) even though he set a single-game school record for passing yards (423).

"It was devastating," says Bevell, "but that game also set us up to refocus for Michigan and Ohio State." The Badgers beat Michigan at Camp Randall, then tied No. 3 Ohio State the following week.

"In my opinion I feel like we beat them in every way, but we had two turnovers in the red zone and they blocked the field goal (at the end of the game). It was bittersweet. There's nothing worse than a tie, but it still kept us in the running."

When Michigan beat the Buckeyes the following week it put Wisconsin back in the driver's seat. The Badgers beat Illinois and then Michigan State in Tokyo for the right to play in the Rose Bowl. Far away from its fans, the team's celebration was exclusive. "There was nobody there but the team. Nobody was running out to go celebrate somewhere else. There was just the team."

"It was the way the season started," says Bevell, "and it was the way it ended at the Tokyo Dome."

While it would have been easy for Wisconsin's players to be glassy-eyed during the trip to Pasadena – the program's first in 30 years – their coach was not about to let them lose their focus. "Coach Alvarez reiterated as we were heading out there that we were in a bowl game, but that not to forget what the ultimate goal was: to win the game," says Bevell. "It was truly the old cliché: one game at a time. We never looked past anybody and this one was just the next one on the schedule."

A television station took Bevell and a teammate to see the ocean for the first time, and he was given an opportunity to meet a boyhood idol, Dodgers manager Tommy Lasorda, one day in practice. The trip was an unforgettable experience for the first-team all-Big Ten quarterback, but on the morning of the game he was all nerves. Then the team bus pulled into the stadium and all Bevell could see was a sea of red – somehow, everything felt fine again.

The UCLA Bruins were favored thanks to a high-powered offense which included quarterback Wayne Cook and All-American wide receiver J.J. Stokes. In his previous 12 games, the 6-foot-4 Stokes had caught 20 touchdowns and was expected to be an absolute nightmare for the Badgers defense. What's more, the team was coached by Terry Donahue, who carried an 8-2-1 bowl record into the contest. And UCLA made sure to tell the Badgers players just how good they were prior to kickoff. "When UCLA came out they were talking all kinds of trouble, trying to mix it up, trying to get us off our game," says Bevell.

But Wisconsin didn't need to engage in any talk; its plan was simple: punch the Bruins in the mouth at the start of the contest and keep punching.

The Badgers moved the ball well on their first series but were forced to punt. On the second series, Bevell completed a first down pass to J.C. Dawkins, then went back to the receiver in the end zone and drew a pass interference call. A few plays later he hit Terrell Fletcher on third and eight for a long gain, setting up Brent Moss' touchdown run to make the score 7-3.

Bevell threw an interception on a tipped pass later in the half but regrouped to guide his club on another touchdown drive before halftime.

"We drove down and missed a field goal that could have put us up even more," says Bevell. "But we were one of those teams that stayed in the moment and knew there was a lot of game left. Everyone was very focused. We knew it was 14-3, but we didn't feel like we had it in the bag."

UCLA began the third quarter with a long, 11-play possession that took them well into field goal range. But Cook fumbled on a play-action pass and Wisconsin recovered. On the Badgers' first play from scrimmage, Fletcher broke free around the right side of the line to take the ball near midfield.

A short time later the team was closing in on scoring range, and Bevell was prepared to execute a play he had planned for all season.

"The whole year, one of my favorite plays was the quarterback throwback – a pitch to the running back where no one covers the quarterback, who runs out the other end and the running back throws him the pass. I worked all year to get the play in and the coaches said, 'No, no, no.' Well, I think I beat them down. Finally one time – and I can't remember if it was coach Alvarez or coach Childress – but they said, 'If we go to a bowl game, we'll put it in for the bowl game.' Obviously, the second we clinched a bowl game I was back up there talking to them. So we put it in for the Rose Bowl and practiced it a bunch with Terrell Fletcher."

After Fletcher fumbled the ball on first down, the coaching staff inserted Moss who picked up a couple of yards on second down. Then, on third down, the coaching staff called for Bevell's play.

"Well, I look and Terrell's not in the huddle. He was the only guy who had worked the play in practice. So he comes onto the field, Brent goes off. Terrell takes his glove off and now the (play) clock is winding down. I'm hustling everyone to the line and right when I say 'hut' they blow the whistle and give us a delay of game penalty."

Bevell would have to wait a few more possessions for his glory. The Badgers turned the ball over on downs that series and lost top wide receiver Lee DeRamus and fullback Mark Montgomery to ejections following a fight that broke out after fourth down.

Cook, who completed his first six passes of the game – all to Stokes – struggled terribly in the second half. He led the Bruins on another 11-play drive, but again the quarterback fumbled the ball away when in scoring range. But Wisconsin went three-and-out and the next time UCLA had the ball it cashed in on a Ricky Davis touchdown run.

When Davis fumbled on UCLA's next possession, the Badgers quickly gained their lead back. A long gain by Moss gave him 100-plus yards for the 11th consecutive game that year; two plays later it was Bevell's turn to carry the football.

"If I remember correctly, it was a four-vertical pass play. We had two receivers to the left and we motioned the fullback out to the right and everyone was to run a go route," says Bevell. "I dropped back and when I got to the back of my drop, for whatever reason there was a hole to the left so I took off running."

As Bevell was making his way to the sideline he recalled advice he'd been given from the coaching staff earlier that year. "I had had a play similar in one of the games that year when I scrambled and kept running sideways and the coaches had told me to get the ball up the field. So on this play I started running left and started thinking, 'I need to get the ball up the field, get the first down, get as far as I can get and slide.'"

But he never had to slide on the 21-yard play. He got excellent blocks downfield from his receivers and even made UCLA defensive back Teddy Lawrence miss before crossing just inside the left pylon.

Described ABC commentator Keith Jackson: "The most unlikely kind of big play – Darrell Bevell *running* for a touchdown."

Bevell's teammates must have agreed with Jackson. "A lot of the guys were messing with me, cracking jokes," says Bevell. "It's ironic that the biggest play of my career was a run."

As bad as it was playing, UCLA was not done fighting. Cook led his club on a long drive later in the fourth quarter, hitting Mike Nguyen for a touchdown. The two-point try failed, leaving the score at 21-16 with little time left.

The Badgers got a pair of long runs by Moss to start the next drive, but a penalty and failed short-yardage attempt forced them to turn it back over to UCLA one last time. "Our last drive, we got the ball with 3:33 to go and we had five runs to try to run the clock out. Our job was to stay on the field and run that clock out and we weren't able to do it," says Bevell.

UCLA started at its own 38-yard line and quickly advanced the ball down the field. In a race against the clock, the Bruins got down just inside the Badgers' 20-yard line before time expired.

Able to exhale, Bevell went searching for someone to celebrate with.

"You're kind of running around for a minute and you don't know what to do," says Bevell. "I remember being on the field looking for every guy on the team."

The Badger offense gained fewer yards than UCLA, and held the ball for approximately the same amount of time by game's end. But it was apparent that Bevell had managed a much better game than Cook had, and that the Badger offensive line had worn down the Bruins defense just as it had planned.

Wisconsin's defense also deserved a tremendous amount of credit for the win. Guys like Lamark Shackerford, Yusef Burgess and Eric Unverzagt had stayed in UCLA's face all evening and helped to cause those six turnovers. And the combination of Jeff Messenger, Kenny Gales and Donny Brady had done well in limiting Stokes to short gains.

In speaking to the *Milwaukee Sentinel* afterward, Bevell admitted it had been a lifelong dream to win the Rose Bowl, only in different colors. "You fantasize about it when you're little and, to be honest, I had dreamed about playing for Arizona State someday in the Rose Bowl," he said. "But I'm on the other side, and it means everything to me."

>>>

The 1994 Wisconsin season was marred by off-the-field issues and another disappointing loss to Minnesota. The team lost big to Colorado but also beat Michigan on the road (the only win in Ann Arbor of Alvarez's career). Still, Bevell and the Badgers posted a 9-3-1 record and a win over Duke in the Hall of Fame Bowl.

In 1995, Bevell's final year at Madison, the team was forced to deal with a large number of losses on offense, particularly upfront. "A lot of the offensive line that had protected me all those years had graduated. It was a whole new crew," says Bevell. "I got beat up a little more, but I could have played better in some games, as well." At 4-5-2 the team failed to qualify for a bowl, and Bevell spent his last night as a college quarterback in the hospital with a lacerated kidney that he suffered in a tie against Illinois.

"It kind of mirrored my last high school game ... both ending in the hospital," says Bevell.

It was almost a given that a career in coaching would follow his playing career. "I love football. I love the game. I had dreamed of being an NFL player, but when I wasn't able to do it I felt going into coaching was a way to stay around the game."

Bevell spent time at Westmar, Iowa State and Connecticut before being offered a job as an offensive assistant with the Green Bay Packers in 2000. Six seasons later he rejoined Childress to become the offensive coordinator of the Minnesota Vikings.

Bevell likes to say, "Who you know can get you the job, but it's what you know that will allow you to keep the job." That has been true of his coaching career and was true of his four years in the lineup at Wisconsin, where he continues to hold every significant career passing record.

TAREK SALEH
1993-1996

The gentleman from Penn State waiting outside wanted an answer. Miles away, Joe Paterno wanted an answer. But Tarek Saleh was still weighing his options.

The Connecticut prep standout grew up watching the Nittany Lions – specifically, the 1986 team that upset Vinny Testaverde and the Miami Hurricanes in the national title game – and had been honored the school wanted him to join their program. But there was something about the University of Wisconsin that intrigued him, something he could not ignore.

"I can remember sitting in my living room debating whether to go to Penn State or Wisconsin," he says. "I knew in my heart where I wanted to go, but when you put things on paper, Penn State was a safe route. All the while I'm doing this the Penn State coach is outside in the driveway. But enough was enough. It wasn't signing day, it was just time to make a decision."

Saleh told the assistant coach he was ready to choose Wisconsin. Surprised and upset by this, the coach told Saleh to call Paterno and deliver the bad news.

"Joe Paterno was a legend – still is – and I have tremendous respect for him ... My dad had given me a cardboard life-size cut-out of Joe Paterno for my room, so Wisconsin had to have something special for me not to go to Penn State. And they did."

Saleh was taken by how head coach Barry Alvarez and assistant coach John Palermo sold their program. Both had an air of confidence, he says, "...and the guys on the team were my kind of guys. Not that the Penn State people were bad, it just wasn't the same."

The product of West Haven's Notre Dame High School, Saleh dressed for three games each week during his first season at the private school – freshman, junior varsity and varsity. "I think Coach (Tom) Marcucci sensed I had something that was different and unique," he says. Saleh started on both sides of the ball as a sophomore and was instrumental in helping the team reach the state title game during both his junior and senior seasons. As Notre Dame's fullback, Saleh gained more than 2,000 yards rushing as a senior and collected more than 50 touchdowns throughout his career. It's no wonder Penn State and Wisconsin were in a tug-of-war.

The Connecticut prep star had committed to a Badgers program that had yet to win its first bowl game under Alvarez ... had yet to accomplish anything of real importance. But the confidence was there – Saleh could feel it – and he was prepared to do all he could to help the program to grow.

Saleh had a part in Wisconsin's 1993 Rose Bowl run and contributed the following year when the Badgers finished 8-3-1 and beat Duke in the Hall of Fame Bowl. His biggest impact, however, came during the 1995 and 1996 seasons, one of the most pivotal times in the progression of Badger football.

The start of the 1995 season was miserable - a 43-7 loss at home against Colorado. "We came back with a young team, whole new offensive line, new running backs, and basically a whole new defense with only a few returning starters," says Saleh.

From there, Alvarez's squad tied with Stanford and beat SMU, 42-0. Still, after three games, 1-1-1 didn't have anyone in Madison excited, and a date with the defending Rose Bowl champion Nittany Lions was up next.

GAME I WON'T FORGET

September 30, 1995
at Penn State

The Nittany Lions made the move to the Big Ten prior to the 1993 season, but the Badgers hadn't played them in either of their first two years in the league. Wisconsin had gotten a taste of Penn State in 1953 and again in 1970 – both UW wins – but this was the first conference clash between the two.

Heading into the contest, the Nittany Lions owned the nation's longest winning streak – 20 games, which dated back to November of 1993. For Wisconsin to snap that streak, in unfriendly Beaver Stadium, would take a near-perfect performance from Alvarez's offense and defense.

Says Saleh, "Coach Alvarez does a great job of preparing his teams for big games and I think his approach was to give them a lot of credit, keep slapping (Penn State) on the back, let them think they were the greatest thing since sliced bread. I remember someone from a Penn State newspaper called me ... I was very polite and respectful. And I was honest about my respect for coach Paterno and the whole team, but in the back of my mind I was thinking that a lot of credit was owed to our team, too. We've won two consecutive bowl games, we have a great program. But I never said any of that, I just complimented Penn State just like coach Alvarez talked about."

Alvarez pushed his guys hard all week on the practice field, and Palermo pushed even harder in the classroom. "He was an intense coach – best coach I ever had," says Saleh. "We had an exam every week, day before the game, and there were a couple of things I got wrong (prior to Penn State) and he just wrote some comments on the test questioning whether I knew what I was doing. Really, I think he was pushing my buttons to piss me off and get me fired up even more for the game. That's why he was so good. Not that I needed much."

After the plane ride into Harrisburg, the Badgers had to take a bus to Happy Valley, where they stayed in a run-down motel. "It was an older place, not very comfortable, so that gets under your skin," says Saleh. "Then, about two in the morning, I couldn't sleep. The Penn State fans were driving around this motel, honking their horns and making noise and I was just staring out the window at them, telling my roommate, 'Man, I just hate this place.'"

The anxiety boiled over prior to kickoff.

"Beaver Stadium is awesome – 96,000 people – they've got that crazy Nittany Lions sound and everything. We go through warmups and the crowd is all around you ... all these frat kids and everyone trying to intimidate you, talking all this junk. It's just a great atmosphere, it makes you want to get after it. Then we got back into the locker room and it was a real shoddy locker room and all of a sudden the power went out, so the lights went out. It pissed us off even more."

"All of that manifested itself in this game."

Penn State had the winning streak, the point spread (-15), the home field advantage, and a more experienced roster. But they didn't stand a chance this particular evening.

From the start, the Badger defense was all over a Penn State offensive attack that included future NFL offensive line starters Marco Rivera and Jeff Hartings. "They had big fullbacks and every time we hit them in the mouth and got after them. It was an all-out effort from a lot of guys who played real hard." The Nittany Lions gained just nine yards on 13 carries in the first half – well off their pace of 290 rushing yards per game.

Trying to keep his guys fresh, Wisconsin defensive coordinator Kevin Cosgrove used a deep rotation up front. Everyone played a role. Says Saleh, "One play in particular, Jason Maniecki pushed back either Rivera or Hartings and grabbed them and the quarterback. That play solidified the defensive side of the game."

The Badgers offense clicked, too. After a 26-yard John Hall field goal, Wisconsin make good on another first quarter drive, this one ending on a 21-yard pass from Darrell Bevell to tight end Matt Nyquist to give the Badgers a 10-0 lead. In the fourth quarter, Bevell led the offense on its biggest drive of the night – a 14-play masterpiece that included four successful third down conversions; Bevell capped that drive with another 21-yard pass, this time to receiver Tony Simmons. Bevell, who completed 18 of 22 attempts, said afterward, "It's one of the greatest victories I've ever been a part of."

Fifth-year senior Michael London had arguably the best game of his career, with six receptions for 94 yards – four of them to extend drives.

The Nittany Lions offense had averaged 49.7 points in its first three games that season; Wisconsin's defense allowed just nine, the bulk of which came on a fourth down pass from Wally Richardson to Freddie Scott with little more than four minutes remaining.

Saleh stood out among a group of defenders who all played well. The junior defensive end produced nine tackles, including two sacks, and was in Richardson's face on several other plays. After the game, Saleh was able to share the moment with those closest to him. "My entire family was there, all of my high school coaches. They all had limited access to seeing me play. It was the day before my dad's birthday. I gave him a poster with a little note, telling him I love him."

The celebration in the locker room and on the plane ride back was more intense. Having constantly been reminded of the loss of 26 seniors from the previous year's team, the 1995 squad and its coaches finally had an opportunity to shrug off all the doubt and dance a little. "We were fired up, high-fivin' and coach gave us 24 hours to celebrate before we got ready for the next game," says Saleh. "Yeah, we partied all the way home."

It was only one win, and there were still seven conference games to be played, but Saleh and the rest of the Badgers knew that if nothing else, they would forever be remembered for pulling off one of the greatest upsets in the history of Wisconsin football.

"You have to give them credit," Paterno told reporters. "They just played one heckuva football game."

>>>

Two weeks later, Saleh and the rest of his teammates returned to Camp Randall to begin the second half of their season. With media talking about a Rose Bowl revival, the Badgers' high hopes immediately came crashing back to earth against the fourth-ranked Ohio State Buckeyes. "We played our asses off but Eddie George broke open a big play. And then we got ambushed in the rain at Northwestern, which was ugly."

The defense helped pull out a win over Michigan State on homecoming ("I think we sacked Tony Banks on just about every down") and two weeks later the Badgers won 34-27 over Minnesota. But that was the end of the celebrating. For the first time in three years, Wisconsin would have to stay home during bowl season. The 4-5-2 record was a disappointment to Saleh, the coaching staff and everyone else around the program.

"I probably played some of my best football in some of those games, even though we lost," he says. "For me, it was my first year of playing at a higher level but it pisses me off looking at this and trying to determine why we didn't do better. I know we were younger and certain things weren't there yet for us to make it happen ... but losing is miserable."

That season did earn Saleh his first national recognition, drawing him a spot on the Big Ten's first-team and an All-American mention from one of the selecting bodies. But the highlight, of course, was that upset win over Penn State. "I think some people say the season was forgotten so this game can be forgotten," says Saleh, "but that's not true of this instance. How well we played ... the game will always be special."

During his senior year in 1996, Saleh broke his own school record for sacks in a single season (14) and became the school's all-time leader in tackles for loss and sacks. That year he captained a squad that earned a trip to the Copper Bowl, where he was named the game's most outstanding defensive player for collecting six tackles and a blocked field goal.

A fourth round pick by the Carolina Panthers in 1997, Saleh played five years in the NFL – two in Carolina and three in Cleveland – before injuries forced him out of football.

"Going to Carolina to play outside linebacker was a pretty big transition for me after having played mostly at defensive end while at Wisconsin," Saleh admits. "There's a huge amount of coverage responsibility. It's a much faster game, more calls, more sophisticated defenses."

The Panthers did not protect him from the expansion draft of 1999 and Cleveland took advantage. There, coach Chris Palmer was convinced by linebackers coach Billy Davis to convert Saleh to fullback, where he played the next two seasons until Butch Davis was hired as the Browns new coach in 2001 and switched him back to linebacker.

"I liked Carolina but I *loved* Cleveland," says Saleh. "It was the perfect situation for me. The people there were great, but we weren't very good."

Saleh also appreciated the experience of playing alongside NFL greats such as Sam Mills, Kevin Greene, Greg Lloyd and Chris Spielman. But by the end of the 2001 season his career had come to an end and it was time to find something new.

In 2003, Saleh accepted a position as the national sales manager for the Madison-based company Impact Sports (now named LIDS Team Sports), which is Nike's No. 1 team dealer in the country and sells apparel and equipment to high school and collegiate teams across the country.

Often, Saleh thinks about the decision he faced as a high school junior – Penn State or Wisconsin – but never with an ounce of regret. "It proved to be a pretty good hunch."

RON DAYNE
1996-1999

High school boys weighing close to 270 pounds are supposed to block for ball carriers, not carry the ball themselves, but Ron Dayne didn't want to hear any of that. All of the college offers were nice, though. Some of the nation's most prestigious schools offered Dayne a chance to play everything from fullback to linebacker. "Notre Dame wanted me as a nose guard," he says, "even though I didn't know how to play it."

Barry Alvarez was one of the few coaches in the country willing to visualize the New Jersey prospect as a tailback, which put Wisconsin near the top of Dayne's list. Even so, he was advised to exercise all of his options.

"My uncle told me to visit another Big Ten team, so I went to Ohio State and on my recruiting trip there six running backs committed. I didn't even get to meet the coach," he says.

Dayne still recalls the first time he met Alvarez. Expecting to visit with the Badgers coach at the school, Dayne instead caught up with Alvarez at his home later that night. "As soon as I came into the house he gave me a big hug. I didn't even know him. It was like I was a son he hadn't seen in a long time."

Thus began one of college football's great player-coach relationships – one that would help to advance the University of Wisconsin's athletic department to new heights and accomplish previously unimaginable things on the field.

From the start of his playing career, Dayne had little trouble mowing down defenders. He was classified as being too big to play before high school, but as soon as he entered Overbrook High School he became a star. That year he figures he scored close to 30 touchdowns for the ninth-grade squad; soon after that New Mexico sent him his first letter.

He couldn't quite get the hang of the shot put so his coach let Dayne take one home to practice. By the end of his high school career he owned the state record in the event and in the discus.

Dayne says the Badgers' 1994 Rose Bowl win wasn't what made him choose the school – just Alvarez's word that he'd get a fair shake to play running back. But even so, no one in the state of Wisconsin expected the freshman would play so soon.

"Coach had told me I'd get a chance but that Carl (McCullough) was the man," he says. The previous year, McCullough had logged 1,038 yards in 10 games, including 100-yard efforts against Colorado and Ohio State. Beyond McCullough, Dayne also had to get by Aaron Stecker, Charles Williams and fellow recruit Eddie Faulkner. It took Dayne a while to crack the starting lineup – five games, to be exact.

After showing considerable results in limited action against Eastern Michigan, UNLV and Stanford, Dayne was turned loose against No. 3 Penn State and the freshman responded with 24 carries for 129 yards and two scores.

No longer 'Ron Dayne, the freshman,' Dayne had become 'The Great Dayne' overnight.

"The only thing I didn't like about it was I couldn't chill – do the stuff kids do when they get to college," says Dayne. "I'd get mobbed when I'd go out."

The rest of the season got even more ridiculous – 30 carries against Purdue, 50 carries against Minnesota, and 41 carries against Illinois; all 200-plus-yard performances, all Wisconsin victories.

If no Big Ten defense could stop the 18-year-old back, certainly Hawaii's Rainbow Warriors had no shot.

GAME I WON'T FORGET
November 30, 1996
at Hawaii

Fred vonAppen's first season as the coach at Hawaii didn't go as planned. The team entered its late November contest with Wisconsin with a 2-9 record, having allowed 34 points and 208.9 rushing yards per contest – numbers that did not match up well against Wisconsin's style of football. The Rainbow Warriors were 27 ½ point underdogs in their own stadium, and all vonAppen could muster pregame was, "We just want to go out and be as competitive as we can and learn from the experience."

As for his gameplan? Even vonAppen wasn't sure. "How are we going to stop Dayne? I don't know."

For Dayne, the game was more than just an opportunity to help his squad become bowl eligible. He entered the contest 93 yards shy of Herschel Walker's national record for freshmen, and 114 yards shy of Brent Moss' single-season Wisconsin record.

But if there was pressure, Dayne and his teammates were too busy having fun to notice. Alvarez allowed his guys to roam the island and have fun in the days prior to kickoff.

Says Dayne, "When we got there Coach gave us freedom to do what we wanted to do. It was almost like a vacation for us. The coaches let us play and treated us like men. It was our responsibility to make sure all the guys were in (before curfew) and we handled it well."

"Part of going to college is having experiences you normally don't have," Alvarez told the media of his team's escapades. "This is part of growing up. I think it's important, and I try to encourage that."

Players rode around the island on scooters, surfed the waves ... some even went snorkeling. Joked Alvarez on mammoth offensive lineman Aaron Gibson's underwater experience, "Gibby may get speared."

By game time, though, Wisconsin was back to business, and Alvarez demanded a fast start. "I realize (Hawaii) has had some problems, but they're going to be emotional," the coach said. "We've got to be able to neutralize that and get a jump on them."

The first drive did not quite go as planned. Penalties were called on the first four snaps, including consecutive false start penalties on Wisconsin. Faced with first and forever, Dayne was given the ball on a clean play and busted free off the right side for 71 yards. Two plays later he bulled his way in for a four-yard score.

Hawaii's best weapon – quarterback Glenn Freitas – did what he could to keep his team in the game on the following drive. The senior signal caller completed several long passes against the Badger defense and got his team to the Wisconsin 19-yard line from where Carlton Oswalt made a short field goal. But Hawaii was only buying time.

Dayne carried seven times on the next drive, capped by his three-yard score. Every time he touched the ball the holes got bigger and bigger, and Dayne gained more and more ground.

"Going into the second quarter, every run seemed like a long run – 30, 40 yards," says Dayne. "After a while I think they got scared of me, and our linemen were huge so they were really scared of them."

On the Badgers' final scoring drive of the half, Dayne took the ball 48 yards for a touchdown on the first play of the possession. The game was only half over and already Dayne had carried 25 times for 250 yards, which broke his own school record for yards in a half. But because the score was 28-10 (Hawaii's touchdown came on an interception return), Dayne's work was not quite done.

Alvarez fed him the ball 11 times more in the third quarter, during which he added another score and 89 yards to his total. His 339 yards broke Billy Marek's 1974 single-game Wisconsin record, and Dayne's 295 carries for the season set another national record among freshman.

Said Hawaii defensive coordinator Don Lindsey, "It was like trying to stop a Mack truck with a pea shooter. It was no contest. No mas."

Fortunately for Lindsey, the Badgers showed mercy; once the team was up 38-10, Alvarez took his freshman out of the game. Recalls Dayne, "I was looking up in the stands, looking to see coach. 'Am I done, or what?' I found my running backs coach and asked 'You talk to coach yet? Am I done?' and he said, 'Yeah, you're done.'"

"We weren't into running the score up, or getting a bunch of yards," says Dayne. "It was just about winning the game."

Wisconsin won alright – 59-10 – and was invited to play Utah in the Copper Bowl. But the story in the papers the next day wasn't so much the team, but rather Alvarez's incredible freshman find.

"To move ahead of the Herschel Walkers and the Tony Dorsetts of the world and not even have started until the fifth game is outstanding," Alvarez told reporters after the game. "I've said all along he's a special back, but this categorizes him as really unique and really special, and someone who has a tremendous future ahead of him."

>>>

Coming off of his record-breaking freshman season (he gained 246 yards and scored three touchdowns in the Copper Bowl), Dayne says he felt very little pressure to duplicate that success the following season. "We played as a team, so it didn't feel like it was all on me," he says. "I knew I had the team behind me."

What happened over Dayne's next three seasons is well documented: he scored no fewer than 15 touchdowns and gained no fewer than 5.2 yards per carry in any one season. In the last regular season game of his senior season Dayne gained 216 yards against Iowa - more than enough to move him past Ricky Williams as college football's all-time leading rusher.

Following the 1998 and 1999 seasons, Dayne and his teammates enjoyed unparalleled success in Pasadena - the running back's proudest team accomplishment. "You don't see teams going where we did," he says, "the only team to win back-to-back Rose Bowls."

In December of 1999, Dayne was invited to New York for the Heisman Trophy presentation. Everyone knew Wisconsin's back - the man whose name Badgers fans and the University's public announcer had chanted loudly and proudly after virtually every first down the past few seasons - was going to win the award, but the anticipation still got to the big back.

"A lot of the guys were like, 'If you cry on TV we're going to get you.' I said, 'Man, there's no way I'm going to cry.'" After hearing his name announced as the Trophy's 1999 recipient, Dayne stood up, shook a few hands and then turned to embrace Alvarez who was seated behind him. "Coach said to me, 'Ronnie, take three deep breaths and you'll be alright.' So I get up there and my eyes were watering and I felt like I was just about to cry so I took the three deep breaths and everything was alright."

Afterward, Dayne asked his coach how he knew the trick would work. "I just knew, Ronnie. I just knew," the coach said. "It was kind of special," says Dayne.

During their four years together, Dayne and Alvarez each helped to cement the other's legacy. Alvarez gave his young back the kind of support he needed, and Dayne gave the program 1,220 carries, 7,125 yards and 71 touchdowns.

Asked if he had seriously considered leaving for the NFL after his third season, Dayne, without hesitation, said he had not. "I had a great four years with my team, and my daughter was born during that time. It was easy for me to stay rather than go to the NFL."

The 11th pick of the 2000 NFL Draft, Dayne found the same level of success hard to come by in New York. The Giants used him to complement their finesse back, Tiki Barber, during his stay in the Big Apple, and Dayne was never given the kind of workload he had come to rely on while at Wisconsin. His number of carries and yards declined in each of his four seasons, and by 2005 the 27-year-old was ready for a fresh start.

"I think if I had had someone like coach (Alvarez), who stuck with the run I may have had more success," says Dayne. Part of the problem was that New York judged him by his size, pegging him as a power back best used in short-yardage and goal line situations – the same mistake colleges had made when he was being recruited. "If they had looked at the film I was never a short-yardage back," says Dayne.

One of Dayne's most memorable performances came on Thanksgiving Day 2005 when he gained 98 yards on just seven carries for Denver in a win over Dallas. Dayne finished his career in Houston and produced the best single-season totals of his career in his final NFL season (2007).

That same year, the University of Wisconsin retired Dayne's #33 during halftime of the team's game against Michigan.

In 2009, former University of Wisconsin Athletic Communications Director Justin Doherty wrote "The Dayne Game," which celebrated Dayne's UW career and the 10th anniversary of his record-breaking 1999 season.

CHRIS McINTOSH
1996-1999

It was the summer after Wisconsin had won its first Rose Bowl, and Pewaukee high school offensive lineman Chris McIntosh was scanning the competition at UW's summer prep football camp when he noticed a 320-pound giant from Indiana named Mike Rosenthal. It had long been McIntosh's dream to play football for the Badgers, but for the first time he was able to visualize the competition that stood between him and that dream. In terms of bulk, there was no comparison; Rosenthal had McIntosh by more than 50 pounds. But as the two went at it throughout the week, McIntosh held his own, punch for punch, through every drill and coaching session.

At the tail end of camp, Badgers coach Barry Alvarez pulled McIntosh and Rosenthal aside and told them both that a scholarship was on the table. McIntosh's heart jumped through his chest; to the best of his knowledge, no Pewaukee player had ever been offered a Division 1 scholarship.

When his mother picked him up, she asked how everything had gone. "I said, 'Oh, it was good. They want me to come play here.' And she said, 'Oh, that's nice.' I said, 'No, they want to pay for my school.' And I'll never forget, she started crying."

McIntosh had plenty of options but gave Wisconsin a verbal commitment before the start of his senior season; that didn't stop a recruiter from Notre Dame from calling once a week. "I told him upfront and he said, 'We don't care if you don't care.' I didn't mind, heck, it was Notre Dame calling."

In Pewaukee's third game that fall, McIntosh blew out his knee. His football season was over, and without having signed an official letter of intent, his future was at risk. "I tore my ACL on a Friday night and the guy from Notre Dame called that Sunday to ask how things were going. I kinda stopped him and said 'Coach, I don't know if you heard this or not, but on Friday night I tore my ACL.' And his reaction was, 'Oh, good luck to you son' and then I heard a click."

McIntosh's knee required four surgeries and a 21-day stay at Mercy Hospital that fall. He contracted a staph infection at one point and was being fed intravenously. The high school senior lost more than 30 pounds in the process. "At one point I remember asking the doctor how quickly I could play – I was young and my priorities were screwed up – and he said, 'I'm trying to *save* your leg right now.'"

The Badgers could have walked away from the verbal commitment but never did. "Barry was true to his word and I came back from it, rehabbed and was 275 or 280 by the time I returned to Madison that summer before my freshman year. I was never as nervous as when I showed up for that first workout."

One thing that had changed from his last visit to Madison was the switch to a new offensive line coach. Bill Callahan had left for the Philadelphia Eagles, and former backfield coach Jim Hueber had replaced him. "I had thought (Hueber) was ... well, outspoken is a nice way of putting it. On the field he's probably the most foul-mouthed, loud and demanding coach you could ever imagine."

During his redshirt freshman season, McIntosh travelled to every game as Wisconsin's seventh lineman. He learned a lot, made mistakes, and caught an earful. "The following year I came in and started at left tackle with four fifth-year seniors and I was the whipping boy – anything that went wrong was my fault. My whole goal was not to screw up. (Hueber) pushed me harder than I had ever been pushed, and he beat me down mentally to the brink."

The verbal prodding escalated to a point where later in his career McIntosh missed a block in a game against Northwestern and got into a shouting match with his coach on the sideline. The next day in practice, Hueber offered his top lineman an apology, telling the other players how much respect he had for McIntosh.

"I've played for a lot of coaches and overall they're not used to admitting when they've made a mistake," says McIntosh. "At the time I found out he was going to be my coach I was almost in tears because I saw how he yelled and how hard he was on his players. But in hindsight I owe him everything. Absolutely everything. He was at my wedding and he's a good friend of mine today."

Following the 1997 season, the Badgers were demolished by Georgia in the Outback Bowl, 33-6. It was one of the ugliest defeats in Alvarez's tenure. A short time later, the coach held a meeting to set the tone for the upcoming offseason.

Recalls McIntosh, "As he leaves he asks if anyone had anything to say. My personality is such that I'm not the most comfortable getting up in front of a lot of people and giving the rah-rah pitch. But it was a moment where no one raised their hand and we all kind of looked at each other and I thought well, you know something needs to be said. We were just at a point where we could have gone either way."

McIntosh made his pitch: "I didn't come to Wisconsin to play in the Outback Bowl," he told the rest of the squad, "I came here to play in the Rose Bowl."

"We had Ron Dayne, who had two years under his belt, we had five returning starting offensive linemen, we had a quarterback in Mike Samuels who was tough as hell; not the most accomplished passer, but he'd come into the huddle after getting his head knocked off, his helmet sitting sideways, and never laid down. We had some great players on defense, we had some good wide receivers ... I said, 'We have all of the pieces in this room. I don't see why we shouldn't be the team that represents the Big Ten in the Rose Bowl this year. I invited everybody who didn't feel that way to leave – nicely – and nobody left. And so that was our goal."

That offseason, McIntosh says the team trained like a Rose Bowl-caliber club, with everyone on the same page. When camp opened in August, the team informed Alvarez of its goal. For three days after every team huddle the Badgers broke with 'Rose Bowl' until one day Alvarez stopped them. "He said, 'You know, you guys don't have the right to do that yet because you haven't earned it.'"

It wasn't long, though, before McIntosh and his teammates did earn that right.

GAME I WON'T FORGET
January 1, 1999
vs UCLA

The 1998 season began as Wisconsin planned it would. Behind a starting line that included McIntosh, behemoth right tackle Aaron Gibson, guards Bill Ferrario and Dave Costa, and center Casey Rabach, the Badgers rolled over the opposition. San Diego State, Ohio and UNLV were little trouble. And despite closer-than-expected games against Indiana and Purdue, the Badgers' record improved to 9-0 by early November. Then the club got tripped up in Ann Arbor, and with just one game left, their goal of finishing the year in Pasadena was all of a sudden in jeopardy.

Facing No. 14 ranked Penn State in a night game at Camp Randall, McIntosh and his teammates got an unexpected boost late in the contest thanks to a suggestion made by former Badgers tight end and UW Athletics Department intern Ryan Sondrup.

"So the end of the third quarter rolls around and this song ("Jump Around") comes on and the whole student section went crazy. I walk out onto the field with all of the offensive linemen and look over at the defensive guys and they're staring at the student section going up and down. I said, 'Look at them, they're (expletive) done. They are done. Now it's time to put a nail in the coffin.'"

Wisconsin 24, Penn State 3. Alvarez's Badgers were finally worthy of chanting 'Rose Bowl.'

Still, even with a Big Ten title and No. 9 national ranking, the Badgers had not yet earned the respect of their opponent, UCLA. Says McIntosh, because the Bruins had been knocked out of the national title discussion they viewed their Rose Bowl berth like a slap in the face.

"We were big underdogs," he admits. "I remember one broadcaster called us the worst team to ever play in the Rose Bowl, so that's the kind of respect we had coming into that game. But we were higher than a kite. UCLA came in dragging their lip, thinking they had been demoted."

But with a lack of respect comes motivation, and UCLA kept throwing fuel on the fire.

"We were at some function with UCLA. My roommate Bob

Adamov and I were sitting on this park bench, waiting for the bus to show up, and (UCLA quarterback) Cade McNown walked by and looked at us and made this flippant comment. He said, 'Don't worry guys, it won't hurt that bad.' I looked at Bob and said 'What the hell did he say?' We were just shocked. I couldn't react to it. Why would you motivate someone like that? Anyway, I came back to practice the next day and told everybody what he said."

Alvarez kept his players focused, never allowing them to lose sight of the team's mission or to believe they didn't belong. "He always talked about having a workmanlike attitude. He's from Pennsylvania, so it was the coal miner-type ethic where you grab your lunch pail and go to work."

At the start of the contest, McIntosh and the other Badger captains were called down to the field for the coin toss.

"They made a mistake and called for us five or ten minutes too early. Normally the national anthem is done and it's just prior to kickoff. So I came out of the tunnel, just a corner of the stadium, and as I was standing in the tunnel all I could see was just the length of one side of the stadium and maybe half of the end zone. It just so happened that that's where all of the Wisconsin people were sitting, all of the UCLA people were out of view. So we're standing in the tunnel with the refs and it was a sea of red and I thought, 'Oh my God, there's nothing but Badger fans here.' They saw our captains standing in the tunnel and a big cheer came down."

"I took my helmet off during the national anthem and they get to 'the home of the brave' and these fighter jets fly over and two go straight and the middle one took this vertical and hit the afterburners and just shook the whole stadium. I'm tearing up as I'm standing there thinking how far I had come from knee surgery to this point. It had been one hell of a trip. I regained my composure, went out to do the coin toss and we started the game."

For Wisconsin to win it needed a heavy dose of Dayne, who was forced to play with a muscle tear near his collarbone. "We needed to run the ball, control the clock, keep their offense off the field, and limit the big play on defense," says McIntosh. "So our offense was our best defense, and their defense was the weak link on their team. In the Miami game they lost they had been run on pretty good. So that's what we needed to do, and frankly that's all we knew how to do anyway."

Like the rest of the world, the Bruins knew Wisconsin's gameplan and hoped to mimic what Michigan had done when it limited the star back to just 53 yards in November. UCLA coach Bob Toledo told reporters that his defenders had prepared for Dayne by tackling a pickup truck in practice. The Bruins may have done better in the Rose Bowl had Toledo not been joking.

McIntosh describes the Badgers first scoring play this way: "On our first drive we ran a stretch play to the left side, my side. I doubled down and Bill Ferrario next to me pulled and the tight end blocked down and we gave the ball to Ronnie. He came around the left side near midfield and the guy I was going against at end was a pretty decent player – he was light, a good pass rush-er – and I got a hold of him and he ended up on the sideline off the field. Literally on the bench. In hindsight it maybe was a bit too much. I think I ran him down our bench. I've got the picture at home. Bill Ferrario's dad gave it to me. It's a snapshot and my guy's on the sideline, Bill is cutting his guy and there's a hole there that – you know how people say a hole is so big you could drive a bus through it? Well, you could literally drive a bus through that hole – and Ron is coming right up through that hole, isn't a guy within 10 yards of him, and he scores."

From there, the back-and-forth battle between two different yet equally stellar offenses began. The Bruins tied the score later in the opening quarter on a 38-yard touchdown pass from McNown to running back Jermaine Lewis. Dayne scored twice more in the second quarter but the Bruins kept pace. "It ended up being a shootout," says McIntosh, "mostly because they had a couple of trick plays they burned us on. There was some fake reverse pass that was perfectly executed so they got a couple of cheap points on us, but we stayed true to our plan."

The two teams again traded touchdowns in the third – Wisconsin's coming on a 22-yard Dayne score and UCLA's on a 10-yard Lewis run. UCLA had moved the ball within a few yards of pay dirt on another third down possession, but a DeShaun Foster fumble gave the Badgers an important break.

As the Badgers offense began to wear down the Bruins defense – as it had done to every opponent that season – the Badgers defense started to play its best football, as well.

The first key play was a Jamar Fletcher interception return for a touchdown to give Wisconsin a 10-point lead early in the fourth quarter. UCLA closed the gap back to seven thanks to a Chris Sailer field goal and gained back the ball in the final minutes of the contest, pinning its hopes on that last possession. But the Badger defense was not about to let the offense down. With 1:07

left and UCLA facing a fourth and three just inside of Wisconsin territory, freshman defensive lineman Wendell Bryant corralled McNown to seal the victory and deliver to Alvarez a second Rose Bowl victory.

"I dreamed about it, pictured it, salivated about it, and I'm just happy to do it," Bryant told reporters of his sack after the game.

Dayne finished with 246 yards – one yard shy of Charles White's 1980 Rose Bowl record – and four scores on just 27 carries. He was unstoppable and well deserving of the most valuable player award.

Caught up in the celebration, McIntosh grabbed hold of the two men who had contributed the most to his football education.

"I was standing there on the sidelines next to coach Hueber. After the game I gave him a hug, turned and there's Barry, gave him a big hug. It brought back flashbacks of the '94 game when I remember those guys jumping around afterwards. It was surreal to be duplicating that. It was one of those times when you look back and realize how far you've come."

"... It was the perfect Barry Alvarez team – an underdog with a chip on its shoulder, getting no respect, running the ball and playing good defense."

>>>

With the bulk of the Rose Bowl team back in 1999, McIntosh and the Badgers decided not to stray from the winning formula. "After break, like the year prior, the goal was the same – do it again."

That year began with sizable wins over Murray State and Ball State before the Badgers hit a wall. The team lost to Cincinnati on the road, then was dealt a Big Ten loss to Michigan at home – McIntosh's fourth and final opportunity to beat the Wolverines.

At 2-2, talk of a Rose Bowl repeat had died.

"So we go to Ohio State and we're down 17-0 at halftime. And now things are really looking bad. Are we taking things for granted? What are we doing wrong? It was not a pretty sight. We got one heck of a pep talk and I think we claimed a chalkboard or two," says McIntosh. "We came out in the second half and beat them, 42-17. That was the turning point for that following season."

Wisconsin beat Minnesota in overtime the following week, then trounced all over Indiana, Michigan State and Northwestern.

Things were tight at Purdue (28-21), but the season finale against Iowa was a cakewalk (41-3). With their 17-9 win over Stanford, McIntosh and the Badgers had accomplished something no other Big Ten school ever had – they won back-to-back Rose Bowls.

And they had earned every ounce of that season ...

"We had to operate from the position of being the favorite the whole time and the pressure was much greater," says McIntosh, who started 50 games during his four-year career. "Throw in a run for the Heisman and Ron trying to break the rushing record ... There was just immense pressure. I'll take that '98 season any day of the week. We were just too naive to know any better."

After college, McIntosh was selected with the 22nd overall pick of the 2000 NFL Draft by Seattle, where he played for the next two seasons.

In his life away from football, McIntosh has used the tools he gained during his time in Madison to build a successful real estate company in the Milwaukee area.

"The five years I spent in Madison have had just a profound influence on my life, without question. The way Barry ran his program, and the things you heard on a daily basis, they were useful in creating a successful football program but they were just good life lessons. I don't know how you get a hundred guys into an auditorium no later than five minutes before a meeting is supposed to start. If you're not five minutes early you're five minutes late, and no one was ever late for a meeting ... and to this day I'm early for everything I go to.

"Everybody bought into the same goal and the same vision. And it's the same thing in my professional life now – concentrate on what I can do, work hard, and have faith that everything is going to work out. For those life lessons I owe a lot to Barry."

NICK GREISEN
1998-2001

Nick Greisen couldn't wait to get onto a football field. From a young age it was what consumed his thoughts and dreams. The good news was that Sturgeon Bay's parochial school offered organized football starting in fifth grade; the bad news was that the Greisen family wasn't Catholic. "We tried to convince my mom to convert," laughs Greisen, "but that didn't work."

Greisen and his family had returned to Sturgeon Bay when he was in elementary school. It was the town where his father had played high school football. "Not a big place, but a place known for football." In the coming years, the small community of 9,000 people would turn out a number of heralded football prospects, including his brother Chris and cousin Casey Rabach.

"Football was something I always enjoyed doing as a kid," says Greisen. "There was no PlayStation or Xbox. I would much rather be outside playing football." Often, he tagged along with Chris and the older kids. "He got annoyed but my mom always made him take me."

In seventh grade, Greisen began his playing career at quarterback, but was dissatisfied by the lack of contact the position provided. He wanted to hit, so he converted to fullback the following season, and stood out at that spot and at linebacker during his four years of high school.

"We didn't have enough guys to have an offense and defense.

You had to play both ways," he says. "And I wanted to be on the field at all times. I wanted to help my team succeed."

The comparisons to his brother never bothered Greisen, even when Chris became one of the state's biggest recruits. "It's something my mom always worried about – me having to grow up in his shadow and him being a four-year starter. But the thing was, he was a quarterback. There was no way for people really to compare us. We played different positions. And I didn't really think about it."

Greisen took up wrestling his junior year because the coach only had seven guys out for the team. He found time for sleep when he could. "I'd go to basketball practice, go home, eat, and go back to weigh in for a wrestling match," he says. As a senior he lettered in five sports (football, basketball, wrestling, track and baseball) and left Sturgeon Bay with a number of school records, including a 46-point performance in basketball. Colleges, however, were all drawn to his ability to play linebacker; more than 100 schools sent Greisen letters of interest.

"My parents believe that if someone takes the time to send something to you, you fill it out and send it back to them. I diligently sat down and filled out every questionnaire." Chris helped his younger brother build a highlight tape and the family sent a professional resume to more than 50 schools. After a lengthy process, it came down to Notre Dame and Wisconsin.

"Every weekend for about two years my parents would go to my games on Friday nights, then wake up early, take a flight and drive for an hour to one of Chris' college games, regardless of where he was playing. I know they enjoyed it, but I just felt Wisconsin would be easier on my parents, plus it was a great school, academically, and it had a great football program."

While attending Badger camp during the summer before his senior year, the prep standout was offered a scholarship. Greisen was all too excited to share the news with his grandfather, who was one of his biggest role models – a 6-foot-5 giant who regularly took him and his older brother Chris to Packer games and who had even been there to help Nick wash his hair in the sink when a shoulder injury prevented him from doing so himself. But his grandfather wasn't available to take the call; he had passed away that same week.

"My family didn't want to pass along the bad news because they wanted me to focus on the dream I was following."

It was a bittersweet moment. His grandfather, who had played briefly for Curly Lambeau's Packers in 1946, had followed Nick's every move – attended every practice, every game. "I felt like he would have given his life to see his grandsons play at a Division 1 college."

Now the dream was his alone, and he was ready for it.

Greisen played most of his freshman season with a torn meniscus. He saw action at linebacker in the second half of the team's game against Michigan after Chris Ghidorzi and Roger Knight were lost to injuries, and again in the Rose Bowl win over UCLA. The following year it was the same story: as he waited his turn behind starting middle linebacker Donnel Thompson, Greisen helped out wherever he could, patiently waiting for his turn.

"My main role was on special teams," he says. "At that time I didn't know if I had what it took to be a starter in the Big Ten, because I hadn't really been on the field much in live action and I was still trying to learn everything."

Greisen and roommate Ben Herbert made a statement by shaving their heads prior to spring practice in 2000. "People had looked at me as this preppy kid who wasn't tough. (The bald head) wasn't a pretty look for me, but everything clicked that spring and the game started to move slower for me. It was the year I found myself as a football player."

Greisen led the Big Ten in tackles and helped his team to the Sun Bowl where they beat UCLA, 21-20. "Most teams would have been happy to go to a bowl game, but after two Rose Bowl games it was almost a bit of a letdown."

An even bigger letdown awaited him and his teammates the following season.

GAME I WON'T FORGET
November 17, 2001
vs Michigan

The 2001 Badgers were a team of puzzle pieces without a clear picture to work from. Freshman running back Anthony Davis was outstanding out of the gate, with four straight performances of 130-plus yards; wide receiver Lee Evans was at his peak and set a school record with 1,545 receiving yards. And yet the team could never put it all together. After beating Virginia in the opener, it lost to a Joey Harrington-led Oregon squad the following week, then to David Carr and Fresno State at Camp Randall the week after that. Both quarterbacks became top five draft picks the following April.

"I think that started us on a downward spin," says Greisen. "We had been used to starting 3-0 and here we were, 1-2."

It also rubbed off in the locker room, he says. "That year we almost had a separation of players and coaches over who was taking responsibility for different losses. That was the hardest part of being a captain and trying to keep your team together. Coaches were saying one thing and it wasn't sitting well with the players."

Wins over Penn State and Ohio State were encouraging; home losses to Indiana and Michigan State were inexplicable. After beating Iowa the Badgers sat at 5-5 with two games to go. Wins would make them bowl eligible; a loss to either club would keep them at home for the holidays, something no Alvarez club had been forced to do since 1995.

The first test was 11th-ranked Michigan.

"We knew we needed a win to remain bowl eligible but this was the University of Michigan," says Greisen. "This was a team that I hadn't beaten in my three years previous there. And it was also senior day, and my last game in Camp Randall. It was a big day for many different reasons ... but our team was ready to play."

The Badgers marched 80 yards down the field on their first scoring drive, finishing on a short touchdown run by quarterback Brooks Bollinger to take a 7-0 lead. Michigan answered back, first on a John Navarre touchdown pass, then on a blocked punt that was returned to make it 14-7 at halftime.

Despite the score, the Badger defense was holding its own and the rushing attack was chipping away at what had been a stout Wolverine front wall. But special teams mistakes continued to make the Badgers pay. In the third, another blocked punt led to a Michigan field goal.

Later in the third quarter, with Michigan leading 17-14, Greisen blitzed and when he smashed into Navarre the quarterback lost the football, leaving it for defensive tackle Anttaj Hawthorne to pounce on. Two minutes later the score was tied.

Both teams stumbled in the final quarter until the Badgers' final drive. Led by Bollinger, the team travelled from its 22-yard line to the Michigan 15 before sputtering with 1:26 remaining. Placekicker Mark Neuser had a chance to be the hero, but his kick sailed right.

"It went from a huge amount of excitement that's balled up inside you ... and then all of that emotion is deflated," says Greisen. "Sixty minutes of hard work wrapped into those few seconds. As a leader and experienced player, you have to tell guys that we need to hold them. And we did that."

Again, the Badger defense kept Michigan in check, and with less than a minute to go forced another punt. Fearing a muffed return, the Badger coaching staff opted to let the punt fall free and send the game into overtime. Apparently, Brett Bell was unaware; the freshman stayed with Michigan's gunner the entire way down the field and when the punt landed it shot straight for Bell, bouncing off his hip before the gunner collected the loose ball at the Wisconsin 13-yard line. A Michigan field goal sealed the 20-17 victory.

"This was the game we needed to win," says Greisen, "and the one that wrapped up the whole season in a nutshell. The ball never bounced our direction that whole year. Who knows had the ball never hit his leg? Would we have won in overtime? Would that have given us the confidence we needed to go to Minnesota the following weekend and get a victory? There are a lot of what ifs."

Wrote the *Milwaukee Journal Sentinel's* Dale Hoffman the day after the game, "In a year when the Big Ten cherishes the average, Wisconsin has been too young or too limited or nagged by too many doubts to take advantage of the league's mediocrity."

"It was very disappointing as a senior," says Greisen. "You'd like to lead guys to more victories, win the Big Ten, but that just wasn't in the cards for us."

The loss was by no means the fault of Greisen and the defense, which held the Michigan rushing attack out of the end zone for the first time that year and limited the Wolverines passing game to 58 yards. Greisen contributed 16 tackles, a sack and a forced fumble.

But numbers mattered very little after the game. "With that loss, nobody wanted to celebrate the Fifth Quarter. That's something I really missed," says Greisen. "With your teammates, with the band. It's a huge tradition and it would have topped everything – to beat Michigan for the first time on Senior Day – and all of those things were taken away in that moment."

>>>

Greisen led the nation with 167 tackles in 2001 and earned a spot on the all-Big Ten team for a second straight year. But all of his success those final two seasons didn't eliminate questions he had about making it at the next level. Greisen pulled himself out of spring classes and moved to Arizona, where he trained for his Pro Day workout with his brother Chris, who had been drafted by the Cardinals in the seventh round of the 1999 NFL Draft.

His agent informed the 6-foot-1, 250-pound prospect that he could be drafted as high as the fourth round in April. Greisen welcomed family and friends to Madison, where they sat patiently on the second day of the Draft and waited for the phone to ring.

"The Giants were the first team to call me," he says. "They were a team I hadn't talked to, hadn't visited." None of that mattered. With their next pick - No. 152 in round five - New York selected Greisen.

"Other than my wedding day and the day my daughter was born it was one of the best days of my life," he says. "It was a reward for all the work that had been dedicated to the sport, not only physically but also the things I needed to do in the classroom in order to be able to compete."

Greisen spent most of his first two seasons in the Big Apple as a backup. He suffered an injury at the start of his third season but later managed to work his way onto the field at one of the team's outside linebacker spots. "A guy was late, didn't do what was expected of him, and coach (Tom) Coughlin ended up sitting him and giving me the start," says Greisen. "I think I had 10 or 11 tackles that game, started the remaining seven games and got to start again the next year." He recorded 60-plus tackles in both 2004 and 2005 but left for Jacksonville in 2006, and then Baltimore in 2007.

"The NFL does stand for Not For Long," says Greisen, "but it's also true that the more you can do, the better off you are." At various times throughout his NFL career Greisen has played on each of the four special teams units, and at all three linebacker spots. "Plus, I picked up long-snapping in case there was ever a situation where the long snapper got hurt, they wouldn't be in a bind."

A knee injury forced Greisen to miss the entire 2009 season and had the 30-year-old contemplating his future, but by spring the next year he had signed with the Denver Broncos and was ready for more contact.

JIM LEONHARD
2001-2004

hroughout the history of Badger football – from that first season of 1889 through its high and low points leading up to the present – there has never been a story quite like that of Jim Leonhard. There have no doubt been bigger players, and stronger ones ... better athletes and even better defensive backs. But never has there been a player who achieved such greatness with so many obstacles to overcome along the way.

At a school known for welcoming walk-ons, no one left Madison walking as proud.

And while sculpting that player took years of hard work and required an impenetrable self-confidence, particularly in his ability to learn everything there was to know before others did, Leonhard's rise from Badger unknown to college football stardom took just a day – an evening, to be precise.

Born into a family rich with coaches of every sort, Leonhard had no way of dodging athletics growing up, nor did he want to. It consumed his after-school and weekend time. He excelled in basketball and on the baseball diamond, and when it was finally time, in organized football.

One thing that helped was having an older brother willing to let him tag along.

"(Brian and his friends) weren't going to cut me any brakes because I was the younger brother or younger than them," says

Leonhard. "I had to grow up. I had to learn on my own."

"When I went back and played against kids my age it was easy."

His father coached him from an early age, and later served as his varsity basketball coach at Flambeau High School. He was more demanding of Jim than any other kid, but ultimately, says Leonhard, "It helped me to get to where I am."

Leonhard's first crack at organized football came in seventh grade. As a freshman he played a small role on Flambeau's state title team. In basketball that year, Leonhard starred in the backcourt for a team that was undefeated through its first 17 games; then Leonhard suffered a broken leg and for the first time in his life had to watch from the sideline.

For some kids, an injury like that awakens them to other opportunities besides sports. Not for Leonhard. It was one of the most anxious times in his life. He couldn't wait to be on his feet and competing again. By his sophomore season he had earned the starting jobs at quarterback and safety in football and was earning a reputation as one of the best players in his conference.

Leonhard credits his head coach, Darrell Gago, and the rest of Flambeau's coaching staff for helping him mature as a player. Those Flambeau teams were capable of putting points on the board, but the other side of the ball is what the school built its reputation upon. "That's when I got addicted to defense. Teams didn't score a whole lot on us, and we took a lot of pride in that ... stopping teams and controlling the game from the defensive side of the ball," he says.

For much of his youth, everyone around him told Leonhard if he could do anything beyond high school, it would be baseball. That was the sport he excelled most in and something that wouldn't require a growth spurt; at 5-foot-8, Leonhard's height had become a liability in basketball and football.

"But the thing was I didn't get that rush. I enjoyed baseball but there was something missing. A feeling I got when I was playing football that I didn't get playing basketball or baseball. And if you quit playing football at the high school level, you'll never play again. You don't get to put the helmet on, you don't get to hit somebody – things you get thrown in jail for outside the game."

During his junior season Leonhard's abilities on the gridiron were starting to draw attention, and it was becoming more apparent that – ideal height or not – coaches were convinced the Flambeau star could play at the next level. Before the start of his senior year, he had been given a piece of advice from University of

Wisconsin-River Falls football coach John O'Grady.

"His recruiting pitch to me was, 'I'm not going to recruit you because you're good enough to play at Wisconsin. I think you need to go to their camp and be seen.' It was the best advice I had ever gotten from anybody. Here's a college coach that's been around for a long time who is running the same system that I ran in high school telling me he's not going to recruit me because I should be at a higher level. It gave me confidence."

At the Badgers camp Leonhard's confidence grew. He took on the best kids from around the Midwest and matched up well with all of them. Still, there was no scholarship offer from Wisconsin, only a preferred walk-on spot. For any other high school athlete it would have been a difficult decision – accept a scholarship to play multiple sports at a Division 2 college, or try to beat the odds at Madison.

For Leonhard, it was easy.

"I felt like if I didn't try, I would have sold myself short, and I wasn't willing to live with that. If I came down here for a year or two, and it didn't work out, I could go to a Division 2 school and still do both. I give my parents a lot of credit. They didn't pressure me into taking the scholarship; they said if you think you can play there, go for it."

From the start he was at a disadvantage; his first year was also the first time the NCAA prohibited walk-ons from participating in summer camp.

"The whole process I had been hearing to come at such-and-such a date in the summer to work out, and then about a week before that date they changed the rules and I couldn't go. I felt like I was already behind. I didn't get to meet the guys, didn't get to meet the coaches. The first time I met anybody was the first day of fall camp."

The only goal Leonhard had that first year was to travel with the team – a lofty goal for a freshman, let alone a walk-on, but Leonhard had gotten used to accomplishing anything he put his mind to.

"We knew that year there was going to be one of us (freshmen defensive backs) that would be playing a lot. It ended up being Scott Starks, but we had no idea at that point. We were all just trying to learn. I just knew I had to get noticed, and I'm not afraid to work hard and do the dirty work. So if it was running down on five kickoffs in a row or something like that, in the coaches' mind it shows them you're willing to do whatever it takes and you're not going to complain about it."

Leonhard caught the coaching staff's attention, and sure enough the kid too small to play Division 1 college football had earned his place as a member of the special teams squad. He travelled to every game.

"It was just another goal. Maybe I was naive at the time, not knowing who redshirts and how much thought goes into it, but it wasn't a big deal to me. I had some success, played a little bit, got beat around a little bit, as most freshmen do ... I had my ups and downs but enjoyed every second of it."

GAME I WON'T FORGET
August 23, 2002
vs Fresno State

Heading into his second season, Leonhard expected to play a bigger role in Wisconsin's defense. Then, almost as if fate intervened, things fell into place for him. Ron Cooper became the team's new secondary coach, and early into training camp starting safety Michael Broussard chose to transfer. Leonhard took the opportunity and ran with it, securing the job in camp. His teammates knew who he was and what he was capable of, but the media and fans knew very little.

"It's funny because I was always a question mark. We had guys coming back, but the safety position was a question mark with this walk-on who had never played a down of defense in the starting lineup. You read all those things and you don't know what to make of them."

To open the season, Wisconsin hosted Fresno State for a Friday evening contest. Night games at Camp Randall offer a jolt of electricity to an already thrilling environment. For Leonhard, the added juice was something he didn't need in his first collegiate start, but shortly into the action all of that didn't matter.

The Badgers got the ball to start the game and drove 54 yards but failed to produce any points. Fresno State quarterback Jeff Grady took over at his team's 43-yard line and threw an incompletion before handing to Matt Rivera for four yards. On third and six, Grady dropped back and looked into the middle of the Badger defense.

"There were some things we tweaked in the offseason, things we changed up from the year before," says Leonhard. "Nothing crazy, but if they had broken down the film from the previous year it was something we wouldn't have done in that situation."

Grady's errant pass ended up in Leonhard's hands and the sophomore returned the ball 25 yards to the Fresno State 32-yard line.

"It always takes a possession or two to get your mind cleared out. To get an interception in that period is huge. Everyone (on defense) is pressing a bit to make that first play, and once it happens everyone settles into their game."

The Badgers scored no points on the ensuing possession, and on the next series Fresno State made them pay with a 22-yard touchdown strike from Grady to star receiver Bernard Berrian. Early into the second quarter the Badgers pounced on a fumble at the Fresno State one-yard line from where freshman fullback Matt Bernstein later pounded the ball in to tie the game, 7-7. A 27-yard Mike Allen field goal five minutes later gave Wisconsin a three-point lead to take into halftime.

More devastating to the Bulldogs that half was the loss of Berrian, who had gained 300-plus all-purpose yards in Fresno State's 32-20 win over Wisconsin the year before. He injured a knee while fielding a punt and never returned. In some ways it only seemed right; the Badgers' top offensive weapon, wide receiver Lee Evans, was resting on the sideline with a bum knee of his own.

The Badger rushing attack was unstoppable for much of the evening, as Anthony Davis (37 carries for 184 yards) logged his seventh consecutive 100-yard game, and Bernstein scored both of Wisconsin's touchdowns – the second coming immediately after a Fresno State touchdown to open the second half scoring.

With Wisconsin leading 20-14 early in the final quarter, Grady threw a second down pass along the right sideline to Adam Jennings that appeared to give Fresno State a first down in Wisconsin territory; instead, Leonhard secured his second interception. "It was kind of a jump ball situation and it's who can make a play, who wants it more. We both caught it at the same time and I came down with it."

Wisconsin again failed to capitalize on Leonhard's turnover and instead fumbled three plays later. With its next possession Fresno State took a 21-20 lead on a 23-yard touchdown pass to Alec Greco.

Badger quarterback Brooks Bollinger then guided the offense to the Fresno State 28 from where Mike Allen lined up for a 45-yard attempt. The kick fell short, but a penalty on the Bulldogs extended the drive and gave Allen another chance from 34 yards out, this one successful with just 2:05 remaining.

"You know at that point the defense is going to decide the game – win or lose. It's crunch time. That's when the big players have to step up," says Leonhard.

Again it was Leonhard who made the big play.

Fresno State began its final drive at its own nine-yard line. After an incompletion, Grady threw three first down passes in a row, first to Deandre Gilbert, then to Marque Davis, then to Rivera. Suddenly the Bulldogs were at the 50-yard line and charging with a minute left on the clock. A penalty and a pair of incompletions put Grady in a fourth-and-19 situation. He dropped back and spotted Davis down the field.

"I got a great read on the play," says Leonhard. "The receiver tried to run an in route in front of me and I got a good break and beat the ball to the receiver."

Turnover on downs. Wisconsin's ball.

"If he catches it, who knows? We win the game," Bulldogs coach Pat Hill told reporters. "But (Leonhard) made the play and we didn't."

By the time the Badgers reached the locker room Leonhard was no longer the question mark in the secondary. He had become dream copy for news guys all over the state – the walk-on who continues to defy the odds. Starks helped feed the story, "Jim Leonhard is a beast. He's a beast. He makes plays. Everything he did today in the game he does every day in practice."

Leonhard kept it all in perspective. "I understood it was only one game. A big game, but only one game."

>>>

In his three years in the starting lineup, Leonhard was never part of a losing team. That sophomore season he grabbed a career-best 11 interceptions. He collected 180 tackles in his final two seasons at Madison – more than any other defender those two years – and left the school with the best career punt return average.

All this and yet as Leonhard transitioned to the next level he again felt unwanted – just another prospect too short and too small to make it in the NFL.

"At every other level it comes down to being a good football player. You might not be the biggest or the fastest, whatever. It always goes back to – if you can play the game you should be out there. Making the jump to the NFL, all you hear is what you can't do. It's crazy how much (scouts) dwell on the negative. You can be a three-time All-American like I was, but it's 'Oh, he's not big enough or fast enough ... solid backup but he'll never start.' I never heard people talk about what I could do – that I had 21 interceptions in college, that I had instincts others didn't have."

Though undrafted, Leonhard received a call from the Buffalo Bills in 2005 asking if he would be interested in trying out for their team as a free agent. In many ways it was Madison all over again, only on a bigger stage, with better athletes. And again Leonhard set goals, and again he accomplished those goals, playing for the Bills for three seasons before spending a year with defensive standouts Ray Lewis and Ed Reed in Baltimore.

Early into his career Leonhard received advice from Buffalo teammate and former Badgers defensive back Troy Vincent. "He taught me the business of football – you work on your weaknesses, but you better never let those strengths slip. Just like in business, those things define who you are. I was never going to get bigger. I could work all day in the weight room, but I knew that size and strength was not going to carry me through ... And after I got that advice, I sat down and thought about it and used it to get better early into my career."

In 2009, Leonhard followed Baltimore's defensive coordinator Rex Ryan to New York, where Ryan had been named coach of the Jets. The team boasted the NFL's top-rated defense, with Leonhard situated as one of its starting safeties. That season the Jets took the league by surprise, winning two road playoff games before losing to Indianapolis in the AFC Championship Game. More newsworthy than the wins, however, was New York's confidence in its defense. The press made it a story, and the Jets players backed up the talk.

"The media looks at you crazy when you speak with confidence and I don't understand that. It's like they expect you to always be humble and never really say how you feel. I saw that in Baltimore. If we thought we were going to win a game, we said so. Heck, I'll predict a victory every game because I believe we can win every game."

It's that confidence that helped Leonhard make it at Madison and in the NFL. And it is what has changed the minds of those who have questioned him along the way.

As Gago once put it to a reporter, "Jim likes a challenge. If you tell him he can't do something ... he'll always prove people wrong."

BRIAN CALHOUN
2005

It's a good thing for Badger fans that Oak Creek's Craig Anderson took the time to talk to his freshman tailback. Friends had convinced Brian Calhoun to go out for the team even though he had never played football before. "I really wasn't feeling it," says Calhoun. "I was debating on whether I should keep playing or quit, and he came up to me and said he had heard I was going to quit and talked me out of it."

Not long after, one of the junior varsity running backs got hurt and Calhoun filled the spot. "The first time I carried the ball for JV I took it 85 yards for a touchdown," he says. "I moved up to varsity by the end of the year and the rest is history."

Oak Creek was one of the strongest programs in the state at the time, having reached the Division 1 title game in 1997 and 1998. But the program had never had a player quite like Calhoun.

As a sophomore, Calhoun gained 1,548 yards on just 105 carries and drew his first Division 1 offer; Iowa had visited the school to scout another player but quickly took notice of Calhoun. The next year he gained 1,967 rushing yards, scored 40 touchdowns and was named the Wisconsin Gatorade Player of the Year. Offers came in from all over, but because he had only lived in Wisconsin for a few years Calhoun did not feel a strong pull to Madison.

Ultimately, he chose Colorado over Nebraska, Tennessee and

the Badgers, in large part due to the good feeling he got from the program's staff. "I wanted to go somewhere where I felt it was home, and had a head coach and a running backs coach that fit my style," he says. The Buffaloes' running back coach at the time was Eric Bieniemy, one of Colorado's all-time greatest players and someone Calhoun instantly clicked with. "That was the guy I felt close to as a mentor and who could take my game to the next level."

Calhoun saw time on the field immediately for Colorado. During his sophomore campaign of 2003, he had 100-yard games against Florida State and Kansas and led the Buffaloes in rushing. But the team finished 5-7 and became engulfed in a number of scandals.

"I enjoyed the two years I was out there," says Calhoun. "But a black cloud had hovered over our football team ... and by that point coach Bieniemy had already left and gone to UCLA."

Upon deciding to transfer, Calhoun worked up a short list of possible schools, which included Wisconsin, Virginia Tech and Tennessee. "Wisconsin was just the best choice because (a) I got a chance to come back home and play in front of a home crowd, and (b) my parents and friends were able to see me play every game. It was a no-brainer."

Because of his status, Calhoun was forced to sit out the entire 2004 season. He helped out as the running back for the scout team and spent the year getting acclimated to campus life at Madison.

"It was an extremely humbling situation because here I came from Colorado where I started and had had a lot of success and all of a sudden I was on scout team," he says. Each week he tested defenders like Erasmus James, Scott Starks and Jim Leonhard in practice – often more than the opposing running back did in the game on Saturday. "It worked both ways," says Calhoun. "They made me better and I helped them prepare each week to play defense."

By the start of the 2005 season, though, Calhoun was ready for his time in the lineup. It was no secret that the transfer from Colorado would do great things for coach Barry Alvarez. It was just a matter of when and what.

GAME I WON'T FORGET
September 24, 2005
vs Michigan

In the season opener, Wisconsin found itself trailing Bowling Green 20-7 early in the second quarter. On the team's second possession, Alvarez decided to feed his new back – first a carry for five yards, then three plays later another for 16, then 4, then 20. The drive ended with a touchdown pass from John Stocco to Jonathan Orr but Calhoun had made his mark. Later in the half it was much the same – five carries for Calhoun on a six-play drive, including a 20-yard touchdown run to put Wisconsin ahead, 21-20. Calhoun added three more scores on the Badgers' next three full possessions and finished the game with 258 yards on 43 carries. Not bad for a debut.

"It was the perfect situation for me to prove I could play and show everyone just a glimpse of what was ahead that season," says Calhoun.

The next week he carried just 11 times in a blowout win over Temple, but made up for it by piling up 171 yards on 38 carries against North Carolina. Life was grand for Calhoun, but as far as outsiders were concerned, the Badgers hadn't beaten a team worth bragging about. "We were 3-0 but we still weren't getting the credit we deserved," he says. "No one expected us to do much preseason, and so here comes Michigan, our first true test. Plus, it was at home and one of our goals had been to go undefeated at home. That wasn't going to change for Michigan or any other team."

The Badger coaching staff also didn't change the gameplan for the nationally-televised night game against the No. 14-ranked Wolverines; on the first drive Calhoun carried on five of the first six snaps and was responsible for three first downs. But the passing game stalled and the Badgers were forced to punt. The Wolverines quickly built a 10-0 lead and it appeared as though Alvarez might be in for a seventh consecutive loss to Michigan.

Says Calhoun, "We definitely were trying to get into a rhythm, and our offense wanted to start off fast. We needed to start off fast. We weren't the type of offense that, if we were down by a lot we could drop back into shotgun and put big points on the board fast. We wanted to establish the run in the first quarter and feel them out."

But Wisconsin's first scoring drive was the product of Stocco's arm more than anything else. The junior signal caller completed four passes for 53 yards before Taylor Mehlhaff put three points on the board.

Trailing 13-3 at halftime, Wisconsin wasn't happy with how things were going. Alvarez stormed into the locker room and demanded his team be more physical at the point of attack. Offensive coordinator Paul Chryst then began to draw up a few plays to feature his junior tailback.

After Wisconsin's defense forced a three-and-out, the Badgers fed Calhoun six times on the next drive, resulting in another Mehlhaff field goal. At the end of the third quarter the Badgers mounted another drive and, again, it was almost all Calhoun – this time eight touches leading to another field goal which trimmed Michigan's lead to four points.

Then the Badgers got their first break of the evening. On Michigan's next possession, running back Max Martin fumbled on second down and linebacker Mark Zalewski scooped up the ball. A personal foul penalty gave the Badgers possession at the Michigan 12-yard line. On his second carry Calhoun got to the edge and crossed the goal line.

"One thing about Michigan's defense was that they prided themselves on being physical and big upfront," says Calhoun. "We had been running the power play successfully, right and left. (The touchdown run) bounced right away and I got a great block from Jason Palermo who pulled to get the linebacker. Their cornerback, Leon Hall, slightly underestimated my speed to the corner. He took a bad angle and luckily I got around him to the end zone."

Michigan's Chad Henne then threw an interception on Michigan's next possession, but Stocco followed suit, giving the Wolverines the ball back with 10:17 left in the game. Three plays later Henne hit wide receiver Mario Manningham on a 49-yard touchdown to give the Wolverines the lead back, 20-16.

The Badgers' next drive stalled, but punter Ken DeBauche pinned Michigan at the three-yard line, and when the defense held it forced the Wolverines to punt the ball to Brandon Williams at midfield. With just 4:29 to go, Wisconsin's offense took control of the ball at its own 48-yard line.

"Everybody was very calm, just wired into doing their job," says Calhoun of the mood at the time. "Stocco was very cool. He never panicked."

Three handoffs to Calhoun and a first down. Three plays later, a nine-yard gain and another first down. Bit by bit the Badgers marched down the field, feeding their back the entire way. After Calhoun caught a pair of nine-yard passes from Stocco to bring the Badgers to the five-yard line the team had a decision to make. Less than a minute remained.

"It's funny," says Calhoun, "because we had just come off a timeout. We're all at the point of exhaustion. We're tired. Coach Chryst says we're going to run the sneak. I thought it was a great play. I knew Michigan thought I would be getting the ball; I think everyone in the stadium thought I'd be getting the ball."

"It was a great call because, quite frankly, Stocco wasn't a great runner."

On third and goal, Stocco snuck up the middle of the defense and found pay dirt. Serving as the decoy, Calhoun came through the line and blocked linebacker Chris Graham to help create an opening for his quarterback. Mehlhaff's extra point made it a 23-20 game with just 24 seconds on the clock. "We were looking for a run but we just didn't get to the ball fast enough," Michigan defensive tackle Pat Massey told reporters. A few plays later it was over – Alvarez's first win over Michigan since the 1994 season.

Calhoun carried 35 times for 155 yards in the victory and led Wisconsin in receiving with seven catches for 59 yards.

Said Alvarez after the game, "He has it all – sprinter's speed, soft hands, and he makes you miss. I don't know that you can find someone who can do it any better than he can."

Even Michigan coach Lloyd Carr had to applaud. "I gained a lot of respect for Brian Calhoun today. He's one tough guy. He keeps coming. He's proved to have incredible endurance and he doesn't fumble the football."

>>>

After having carried the ball 127 times in his team's first four games there were doubts as to whether Calhoun could hold up. Asked *Milwaukee Journal Sentinel* reporter Mark Stewart in a column, "But Calhoun can't keep up this work load, can he?"

Not quite, but close. Calhoun averaged 24.5 carries per game the rest of that season and totaled 2,207 yards from scrimmage. His 24 touchdowns also broke Ron Dayne's single-season school record.

But even Calhoun was little help in November games against Penn State and Iowa. Those losses knocked Wisconsin out of contention for the Big Ten title. Still, the 2005 squad had greatly exceeded preseason expectations and had earned a spot in the Capital One Bowl, where they beat up on a heavily-favored Auburn squad; Calhoun had 213 yards in that contest and was named its most valuable player.

Says Calhoun, "Looking back at the season, we were excited to finish 9-3. Penn State was a big game, but they were probably just a better team than us. And Iowa was frustrating. But I think everything was salvaged when we beat Auburn in the bowl game."

The end of the year presented Calhoun with another difficult life decision. Ultimately, he chose to leave school a year early and head for the NFL, where he became the Detroit Lions' third round choice in the 2006 Draft. The Lions were well stocked at running back when Calhoun arrived, and in 2008 the team added Kevin Smith. After three years Calhoun left for a spot with the Canadian Football League's Hamilton Tiger-Cats.

"Playing in Detroit was a unique experience and I'm thankful for it," says Calhoun. "Now I'm just trying to find my way back."

"Football is a part of my life and will always be a part of my life, whether I go into coaching or broadcasting. I'm excited for the future but I'm also excited for where I'm at now."

Calhoun believes every stop of his football journey has served a purpose in his growth as a person, but he admits he sometimes cannot believe how profound his impact was at Madison in just one season of play.

"To this day people still come up to me, or email me, to tell me they enjoyed watching me play at Wisconsin," he says. "I look back and sometimes think I should have just come to Wisconsin in the first place, but I enjoyed the experience I had at Colorado and the process it took to get me back to Wisconsin. It's an experience I will cherish for the rest of my life."

JOE THOMAS
2003-2006

Growing up, Joe Thomas always towered over the other kids in his class.

"I was probably 6-2 when I started in seventh grade, 6-4 by eighth grade, and by the time I was a freshman I was 6-7," he says. But Thomas had all he could do to keep weight on – a problem that stuck even into his early years of college. "It made me think I was going to be a basketball player growing up because I was so tall and thin."

In some ways, it all was a blessing in disguise. Basketball gave Thomas the quick feet that would later help to distinguish him on the gridiron. "I was always expected to be quick, agile and athletic," he says. "It's not that if you start as a lineman you're not expected to be those things, but that developed my footwork and ability to move. And as I filled out I was able to keep those things."

The oldest of three children – all spaced comfortably apart – Thomas vividly remembers following the 1993 Badger squad during its journey to the Rose Bowl ... the excitement, the hoopla, and how it changed the attitude people from his hometown had toward Wisconsin football.

As a seventh grader, Thomas played fullback for the Junior Lancers program. "By eighth grade they moved me to tight end and outside linebacker and that's where I stayed until my senior year of high school," he says.

As part of an athletically-gifted class that included future Division 1 athletes Ben Strickland, Steve Johnson and Luke Holmen, Thomas and his teammates tore through everything they played. He stood out in AAU hoops and was the goalie for the state champion select soccer team.

But in high school, it was Thomas' accomplishments on the football field that drew the attention of scouts all over the country. On defense, he dominated. After switching from tight end to tackle his senior year, he dominated. Bit by bit he was developing into one of Wisconsin's finest prep players; it also didn't hurt that one of Brookfield Central High School's assistant football coaches was 1993 Badger co-captain Joe Panos.

Panos had Big Ten and NFL experience that no other Brookfield Central coach brought to the table. He helped Thomas with his technique and proper footwork. More than anything, he gave Thomas confidence that he could succeed at the next level.

"Growing up, there are dads and coaches telling you how good you are and that you can play ball, but you don't really know because they don't have any credibility. They've never been on that level. When Joe started saying those things I began to believe that I did have the necessary skills to play college football."

But Thomas says Panos did not meddle when it came time for the highly-touted prep prospect to choose a college. Thomas explored every option, and turned to Panos for advice on occasion.

"My recruiting process was long and drawn out. At the beginning I didn't know if I wanted to stay home or not, and Joe was a big help. He was very neutral and told me what he thought was important about picking a college. Never once did he say 'You need to go to Wisconsin.' But after going out and seeing other schools I was able to see how great it was at Wisconsin."

Thomas' first goal once he landed in Madison was to add weight to his frame; at 250, he was terribly light for a Big Ten tackle.

"It's always a chore and a battle. I knew I could play at whatever weight I was at, but also that I would be better with more weight. So I was eating everything I could, drinking every protein shake you could think of. The meals almost became a hassle because of what I was trying to get into my body three or four times a day."

In that first season, Wisconsin played Thomas at tight end – really as an extra tackle – to help their blue chip recruit gain experience. By year two the big guy from Brookfield was filling out and playing full time, but not without a few growing pains. "We played Northwestern and I repeatedly screwed up one of our best plays. Our bread and butter," he says. "I think I screwed up the call six or seven times, which is an incredible number of mental errors for one game. I remember sitting in the coach's office being asked if everything was ok, if they were throwing too much at me, because it was such a simple play. I didn't have an answer. I still don't. It was just one of those things you go through, growing pains."

There were few days like that one; Thomas had earned the respect of Barry Alvarez and the Badgers' coaching staff and was ready to make a name for himself in 2005.

Then, in the weeks leading up to his junior season, Thomas and his teammates were called into the McClain Center where Alvarez announced it would be his last season and that Bret Bielema would take over the program.

"We were all shocked, but it sunk in after that and we all just kind of knew we had better make it a good year to send Barry out because he had been such a good coach, had been so good to all of us, and we wanted to be known as a class that gave him a fitting end to his career."

GAME I WON'T FORGET
January 2, 2006
vs Auburn

Even at the start of the 2005 college football season there were whispers that Thomas might take his game to the NFL in 2006. He had the size scouts desired, and few defenders had gotten the best of him on Saturdays. Even Michigan's outstanding pass rusher, LaMarr Woodley, couldn't get past Thomas. "He was the bad ass in the conference and was killing people," recalls Thomas. "I watched a lot of film on him and dissected things and played extremely well. He didn't even get a sniff of the quarterback. There was nobody really who gave me fits."

But Thomas took each game as it came, and did his best to avoid the NFL hype.

"I never looked at it as 'I've got to make it to the NFL.' I didn't think about it. I was just trying to enjoy the experience and get better at my position and become a great left tackle. It wasn't until midway through that season that it entered my mind." Thomas took a call from former Badger lineman Dan Buenning, who was in his rookie year with the Tampa Bay Buccaneers. "He told me their coach or scouts had told him I was good enough to be a late first round pick. It knocked me off my feet. I thought I was alright, but I had no idea how I would translate or if people thought I could play."

"As the year was coming to a close I knew I would have to make a decision, because people were asking me all the time."

After an 8-1 start, things cooled for Thomas and his teammates; they lost in back-to-back games against Penn State and Iowa. With the third-best record in the Big Ten, Wisconsin had earned a chance to play against Auburn in the Capital One Bowl. It was a considerable upgrade from where preseason prognosticators had picked Wisconsin to finish. "Brian Calhoun had an outstanding year, and John Stocco did a great job throwing the ball that entire year," says Thomas. "People didn't give us much credit but we had a decent season."

Heading into the bowl game, Wisconsin received almost no respect. Across the board, analysts talked of how Auburn was the dominant team, and how the SEC was the dominant conference. Wisconsin, they all figured, didn't stand a chance.

Recalls Thomas, "The bowl preparation was typical Barry – a lot of long, hard practices. We started practicing with the scout team as soon as we knew who the opponent was. A lot of other teams wait for the week of the bowl and treat it like any other game. Barry wanted us to know the opponent inside and out. So we had three weeks of practice against Auburn before we went down there to play the game."

Never did Alvarez play up the fact that it would be his last game. And as best Thomas remembers, the coach never spoke of it after that meeting in August. But if Alvarez wasn't willing to use his exit for added motivation, he was happy to play the underdog card.

"He would always bring up quotes in the paper if the opponent had said something overly confident or cocky, and that nobody felt we had a chance against the big, bad mighty SEC teams," says Thomas.

"We came in with quite a chip on our shoulder. We wanted to prove to everybody that just because we didn't have as many paper athletes who could run fast and jump high that we were just as good, if not better, football players."

Thomas had faced Auburn once before, in the 2003 Music City Bowl following his freshman season. In that game defensive line coach John Palermo stuck Thomas in for a few plays on defense. The Badgers were thin up front, and Thomas was happy to see the extra time. Wisconsin lost that game, 28-14.

Fast forward to 2005 ...

"It had become a running joke all season. I'd go up to (Palermo) and say, 'Hey, if you need me I'm still here, I can play defense.' As we're doing the bowl prep, he approached me and asked if I'd mind stepping in on defense. They were thin and dealing with some injuries and I thought, 'Yeah, I'd love to get a couple of snaps in, have some fun, and help the team win on defense.' And I knew Auburn wouldn't have any clue what my strengths or weaknesses were."

Alvarez gave his blessing for Palermo to use Thomas, so long as it didn't affect the team's left tackle at all on offense.

Neither Wisconsin nor Auburn moved the ball much on their first couple of series. Then, midway through the first quarter, the Badgers took over at their own 25-yard line. Stocco hit Brandon Williams on a 17-yard completion. Then Calhoun cruised for 28 yards, followed by a 30-yard touchdown pass from Stocco to Williams. The 57-second drive gave Wisconsin a 7-0 lead. Kicker Taylor Mehlhaff added a field goal on the team's next possession to give the Badgers a 10-point cushion.

Near the start of the second quarter Wisconsin orchestrated another long drive. Stocco was five for five on the possession, capped by his 13-yard scoring strike to tight end Owen Daniels. With a 17-0 halftime lead, the Badgers were not the least bit intimidated by their SEC foe.

Much of Calhoun's success that afternoon was the product of offensive coordinator Paul Chryst's design. Chryst had observed how Auburn's quick linebackers often over-pursued the ball carrier. He used their speed against them.

"He was a brilliant offensive coordinator," says Thomas. "He put in a play called scissors – a zone play to the right or left that tries to get the linebackers and defense to flow that way, and then the running back puts his foot in the dirt, pivots and the quarterback gives him the ball going the other way. Basically you're trying to circle the defense. If you have a running back that's fast enough it's a very effective play, especially if the opposing linebackers are a little anxious and over-running the play like Auburn's linebackers were."

All day long Calhoun torched the Tigers, collecting 213 yards on 30 carries in his MVP performance.

"For a team that was supposed to be slow and over-matched, we beat them at their own game," laughs Thomas.

In the second half, Palermo felt the need to call on his secret weapon. For a few plays Thomas felt great and performed well. Then his career flashed before his eyes.

Thomas recalls the play: "It was a toss sweep to the other side away from me. I was playing left defensive end and it went over our right side. I locked up with the offensive tackle and shed the block, and the play ended up going for a 10- or 15-yard gain. I remember turning and starting to pursue to get in on the tackle from behind. The angle I was taking had to be reduced. Basically, running full speed I planted my right foot to try to make a quick stop, a change of direction, and as soon as I did it popped on me. I took a couple more steps and fell to the ground. I had never really been hurt in my life, but instantly I knew."

All that went through Thomas' mind at the time was what his injury would mean to the offense. Leading by 14 points, the unit would have to turn to redshirt freshman tackle Eric VandenHeuvel. "He didn't have much experience and Auburn had a few good defensive ends. I'm thinking, 'Look what I just did. I got hurt playing defense and my team is going to need me on offense and I'm not going to be there.'"

VandenHeuvel performed well and Wisconsin held off Auburn's second half charge. Calhoun's 33-yard touchdown run early into the fourth quarter gave Wisconsin a 24-10 lead, which they kept for the rest of the game.

It was a bittersweet moment for the team's junior tackle.

"After the game I was sitting in the locker room with my parents and the doctor had said he thought I tore my ACL. (Palermo) was really shook up about it. He is as rough and tough as they come, but you could see he was tore up. He started apologizing profusely. I didn't know anything about modern medicine. I thought maybe it was all over."

The day was everything Badger fans hoped it could be for Alvarez – his eighth bowl victory to highlight an amazing 16-year run. As the outgoing coach was brought to the stage to accept the Capital One Bowl trophy, Thomas was propped up by a pair of crutches, off to the side of the celebration. "I was ecstatic we won that game and happy for Barry," he says, "... but crutching back into the locker room the reality sunk in that I had a long road ahead of me if I wanted to play football again."

>>>

With his career in jeopardy, the idea of leaving school early for the NFL was no longer an option. Not that Thomas was ever all that serious about it to begin with. "I loved Madison. I loved playing for the Badgers. Obviously playing in the NFL was a dream, but it was something I was willing to put on hold, even if I hadn't gotten injured."

Draft analysts informed Thomas that he would have been the second tackle selected had he left school early, probably a mid- to late-first round pick. The decision to stay paid huge dividends, though. Thomas had an outstanding senior season as part of a team that lost just one contest in Bielema's debut. For Thomas it led to a second-straight all-Big Ten selection and a spot front and center at the 2007 NFL Draft.

"I think it can be said for anybody coming out, unless you're going to be a top five pick it doesn't make sense to leave for the NFL Draft early. If you can move from 20th to fifth, or even higher, it's a huge difference in the value of your contract."

For Thomas that difference helped to make him the third overall selection to Cleveland – the highest a Badger had ever been selected. But while his peers were in New York City eating up the press, he was on a boat in Lake Michigan, fishing with his father and Panos. No big-time prospect had ever shunned the NFL limelight like that before, but for Thomas it was just him being who he is.

"I remember watching Aaron Rodgers slip (to the 24th pick) a couple of years before and it looked like he was having a miserable time, like he was just awful," says Thomas. "Watching that, I was thinking to myself that none of it looked fun. I couldn't imagine why anyone would want to go to it. And talking to my agent I learned it was really just a four-day dog and pony show where the NFL drags you around to 700 autograph signings, and you have to wear a suit, and all that. It didn't appeal to me at all."

But after the boat docked Thomas got back to business. After landing in Cleveland, where Browns fans welcomed him with open arms, Thomas produced one of the finest seasons ever by a first-year offensive tackle. At season's end he was in Honolulu, lapping up the sun and all of the accolades. Minnesota running back

Adrian Peterson won offensive rookie of the year honors that season, claiming 46 ½ of the 50 votes cast; Thomas was the only other rookie to claim votes.

Thomas has earned a trip to the Pro Bowl in each of his first three seasons, making him one of the most successful Badger players to transition to the next level.

TYLER DONOVAN
2004-2007

Following a season in which Wisconsin set a program record with 12 wins in coach Bret Bielema's debut, the talk around Madison heading into 2007 focused on who the team would be able to count on to replace its three-year starter at quarterback, John Stocco.

The Badgers had two likely candidates – long-time backup Tyler Donovan and Kansas State castoff Allan Evridge – and reports from spring camp had the two neck and neck. But to outsiders, the competition represented what would be the team's ultimate downfall in 2007; most believed that neither Donovan nor Evridge possessed enough of what it would take to make the team competitive.

But, then again, few knew Donovan well enough to assume such things, and after the 6-foot-1 quarterback moved past Evridge he quickly took command of the offense. Donovan had spent much of his life building toward the opportunity, and there was no way he was going to let it slip from his grasp.

"I was the backup for three years, playing behind a guy that didn't lose many games. Going into my senior season, I felt it was my job, my opportunity, and my role to take over," says Donovan. "My teammates needed someone to rally behind and I took the role and went with it. There was never really a doubt in my mind ... I knew I would be a leader and playmaker for the Badgers."

Originally a running back in Brookfield's youth football program, Donovan was one day encouraged by a coach to try his hand at quarterback. "As soon as I started playing football there was something different about the game from a competitive standpoint. The quarterback position fit my tangibles and what I was looking for in the sporting world."

When Donovan was ready for high school, he switched schools to Hartland Arrowhead, where he had the opportunity to learn from legendary coach Tom Taraska.

"My family knew it would be a great program to grow in and play for a great coach who knows how to turn athletes into football players," says Donovan.

During his senior season, Donovan completed 99 of 171 passes for 1,650 yards and averaged more than 10 yards per rushing attempt. He guided Arrowhead to the WIAA state title game where it lost to Marshfield, 20-14. "My game in High School was very similar to my game in college, in that I would play the game to my strengths. Having the ball in my hands and being in the position to help win games was what I thrived off of."

Donovan was one of the top-rated prospects in the state of Wisconsin, but he didn't make the Badgers fight off other schools for his services. "I grew up around the program, always a Badger at heart. As soon as they popped into the equation, offering me before my junior year, it was a no brainer for me."

If he was anything during the early part of his career, Donovan was patient. He waited his turn behind Jim Sorgi and Stocco, and then made the best of the situation when coach Barry Alvarez retired and Bielema took over.

"Throughout the recruiting process, I was expecting to play for coach Alvarez during my time as a Badger, but just like any university things can change. That's college football," he says. "I had always had a strong relationship with coach Bielema and everything went very smooth with coach (Paul) Chryst coming in as my position coach. We gelled well as a group. I understood what they needed from me as a leader of the team. They always put me in position to win games and I believed in them."

In his junior year, Donovan came in for an injured Stocco and helped Wisconsin defeat Iowa, 24-21, then Buffalo, 35-3. In the two contests Donovan was incredibly efficient, completing 33 of 50 passes with four touchdowns and one interception.

"A big part of my game was perseverance – always staying mentally sharp ... being ready for my time to lead the team to victories."

GAME I WON'T FORGET
September 8, 2007
at UNLV

Ready? In the 2007 season opener against Washington State, Donovan proved more than ready. The senior signal caller was near flawless, completing 19 of 29 passes for 284 yards and three touchdowns. His one-yard scoring run in the fourth quarter capped a 42-21 win.

Bielema shared with reporters one thing that impressed him about Donovan's showing. "He said, 'We left some things out there today.' So that tells me he's going to be his own worst critic."

Next up for Wisconsin was a trip to Nevada, where they were to face a quick and athletic UNLV squad.

"We knew it was going to be a different environment than playing in Madison, and that the heat would certainly be a factor," says Donovan. "And I still had some proving to do in terms of showing I could be a capable starter on the road."

The Badger coaching staff fully anticipated UNLV's defense to be aggressive, especially on obvious passing downs. They would test the Badgers' new starting quarterback, and it was up to Donovan to make them pay. "They were fast and athletic. A little undersized in the secondary, but big upfront," recalls Donovan. "We knew they liked to bring the blitz a lot, so there were a lot of hot reads that needed to be made in that game."

Wisconsin would have to play the game without its shifty running back Lance Smith, who had been suspended prior to the start of the season. As part of the arrangement, Smith was not permitted to travel to road games. "Not having much depth at the running back position was going to hurt. But I obviously felt good with P.J. (Hill) in the backfield and my receiving corps was really starting to develop as a group."

On UNLV's second drive, quarterback Travis Dixon completed six passes, including a five-yard touchdown to Casey Flair to give the Rebels the first score. Donovan and Wisconsin answered with a seven-play scoring drive – six runs followed by a four-yard touchdown pass from Donovan to tight end Garrett Graham to tie the score at 7-7. Hill gained 40 yards on three carries on the drive – part of a 30-carry, 147-yard effort for the sophomore.

Near the end of the half, Wisconsin conducted another scoring drive, this one taking better advantage of Donovan's arm. On a third down and one at the Badgers' 18-yard line, Donovan connected with tight end Travis Beckum for a 24-yard gain. Then on second down he hit Luke Swan for 18 yards, and then for 16 more on the very next play. In all, Donovan completed six of nine passes on the drive for 86 yards. Taylor Mehlhaff's 27-yard field goal gave the Badgers a 9-7 lead at the half.

"They weren't playing timid by any means," says Donovan of the Rebels defense. "They were intent on bringing the blitz on any passing situation. But we knew as long as we took care of our business there would be opportunities there for us."

Wisconsin mounted a 12-play drive to start the second half, but Hill was stopped on fourth and one and UNLV capitalized by marching down the field for a 25-yard field goal.

At the start of the fourth quarter a Dixon pass was intercepted by Wisconsin safety Shane Carter, who returned the ball all the way to the UNLV 39-yard line. From there Mehlhaff hit a 51-yard field goal, only to watch as another UNLV field goal gave the Rebels a 13-12 lead a short time later.

"It was one of those games where both offenses were moving the ball, but both were having trouble punching it in," says Donovan. "We were having success in the passing game, a couple of big third down conversions, and nitpicking them down the field."

But it had been enough nitpicking; it was time to put the game away.

On the Badgers' next possession, Donovan would define his season – and Badger career – on a 10-play, 61-yard scoring drive. On third and two at midfield he hit Swan for six yards to extend the drive. Then Hill took over for a while, gaining 22 yards on five carries over the next six plays, one of which on fourth and one.

"I remember that drive being a situation where we weren't going to let this non-conference game put a damper on our season," says Donovan. "You could see it in everyone's eyes in the huddle."

The Badgers slowly marched down the field as the minutes ticked off the clock. Then, suddenly, Donovan got an idea.

"The emphasis was to run the ball with P.J. on power plays – traditional Wisconsin stuff – and at one point coach Chryst had observed that UNLV's defense wasn't keeping their eyes on me on that power play. I think we ran it five times in a row and then I suggested 'Let's get them on this.' We called a timeout, coach Chryst agreed, and we caught them off guard."

On first and 15 from the UNLV 29, Donovan motioned the tight end to the right, then faked to Hill and bootlegged to his left. He ran around crashing linebacker Starr Fuimaono and started sprinting down the left sideline. As he approached the pylon he was met by two defenders. Donovan dove, reaching the ball just inside the end zone for the game-winning touchdown – an image fit for a poster.

"We didn't even tell the offensive line. They thought it was just power. The only people that knew were the receivers and P.J.," says Donovan. "Everyone did their part on that drive and (Swan) made a block downfield, which did spring me to the far left side."

"That's what it's all about – those situations," he says. "I wanted the ball in my hands and there wasn't anything that was going to keep me from the end zone."

With less than two minutes to work with, UNLV had little hope. Jason Chapman and Kirk DeCremer each sacked Dixon on the Rebels' final possession, which ended on a fourth down incompletion. Donovan kneeled down three times to close it out.

"He's a heck of an athlete," said Carter of Donovan's touchdown run. "A lot of quarterbacks across the country can't do that."

>>>

After Wisconsin secured an easy win over The Citadel, Donovan led the offense to 10 fourth-quarter points in a 17-13 win over Iowa, then to a 37-34 win over Michigan State. Suddenly, the Wisconsin team that had entered the season with a big question mark at quarterback was 5-0 and in the thick of the Big Ten title hunt.

But the first real setback of the season – for both Donovan and Wisconsin – came the following week against a loaded Illinois club. Despite passing for a career-high 392 yards, Donovan threw an interception in the fourth quarter that helped Illinois extend its lead. The following week Wisconsin lost another game, this time to Penn State, 38-7.

As the season progressed, injuries began to impact the offense, as the team lost both of its starting wide receivers and Hill. To replace them, Wisconsin was forced to turn to a number of freshmen with limited experience. Donovan was one of Wisconsin's few constant performers. "I made sure I was a leader to help the younger guys step up and play," he says.

Donovan played very well the rest of the way, especially in Wisconsin's 37-21 win over Michigan during which he passed for

245 yards and a touchdown, and rushed for 49 yards and a score on six carries. In the bowl game against Tennessee, Donovan passed for a score and rushed for another, but it was not quite enough in the 21-14 defeat.

With a 9-4 record as a starter that season, Donovan had far exceeded what had been expected of him entering the year.

He played briefly for the Edmonton Eskimos of the Canadian Football League before joining his hometown Milwaukee Iron of the Arena Football League. In six games he completed 72 of 142 passes for 875 yards and 12 touchdowns. "It was a fun experience and was nice to be close to home again," he says.

Donovan now works for International Capital Investments Company in Chicago, assisting clients on decisions regarding a variety of investment options.

He says he took more from his experience at Madison than he ever could have imagined.

"The game and the things you learn through the program – things coach Alvarez and coach Bielema taught – are things you take with you for the rest of your life," says Donovan. "You don't think about it much when you're a student athlete, but when you get out into the real world you see it."

"Between the lines and outside the lines there are things I learned through five years of Wisconsin football that have helped me become a better person."